OSPREY AIRCRAFT OF THE ACES® • 80

American Spitfire Aces
of World War 2

SERIES EDITOR: TONY HOLMES

OSPREY AIRCRAFT OF THE ACES® • 80

American Spitfire Aces of World War 2

Andrew Thomas

OSPREY
PUBLISHING

Front Cover
Following three years of bitter fighting between Axis and Allied armies in North Africa, by early May 1943, German and Italian forces in-theatre were trapped in northeastern Tunisia. On Thursday, 6 May, a direct assault on Tunis began under heavy air cover. Axis fighters continued to oppose the RAF and USAAF, and a series of dogfights were fought through the day. In the late afternoon, Spitfires of the 31st Fighter Group (FG) mounted a sweep, with one of the aircraft (Spitfire VC ER187) being flown by newly-promoted Maj Frank Hill of the 309th Fighter Squadron (FS). He had 'made ace' during a mission earlier in the day, and at 1600 hrs he led his flight into an engagement with enemy fighters over Tunis;

'We ran into about 16 ME-109s and Macchi 202s. There were six of us in Spit Vs and four above us in Spit IXs. I started after this formation, came up from underneath where they didn't see us and shot at one Macchi, which I hit. He immediately half-rolled and started down. I don't know if he crashed or pulled out. I just damaged it. Their formation then split up, and so did ours, and we fought a general dogfight.

'Maj Kelly, who was a new replacement, was my wingman. He stayed with me, even though he lagged behind a couple of times, because he was in a much slower aeroplane. When we sighted some more ME-109s and gave chase, two of them turned off and climbed into the sun. We went after them, underneath and behind, so they didn't see us. When we were able to close in again, I opened fire on the lead one when they both half-rolled, and he went down trailing glycol and smoke. Maj Kelly watched him for a long while, and believed he never did come out of the dive.

'The other ME-109 straightened out right away, and I came up on his tail and fired what little ammunition I had left at him. Kelly shot at him too, and then we both broke away. The German must have known I was out of ammunition, because he turned right back and started after us. He was almost on Kelly's tail when I told my No 2 to break hard left. The ME-109 overshot us and never did attack us again. We were down to our last few gallons of gas, so we landed at an emergency field near the front, re-serviced and came on home.'

Although Maj Hill had identified both Macchi and Messerschmitt fighters, his flight had probably engaged 14 Macchi C.202s of 7° *Gruppo*, which had in turn made a number of claims. The Italians lost Capitano Sergio Maurer, and the *Gruppo* commander, Tenente Colonnello Giovanni Zapetta, crash-landed. Maj Hill was duly credited with a Bf 109 destroyed and a C.202 and a second Messerschmitt fighter damaged. He had thus made a significant contribution to the 31st FG's claims for the most fighters destroyed by an American fighter group in a single day in the North African theatre (*Cover artwork by Mark Postlethwaite*)

First published in Great Britain in 2007 by Osprey Publishing
Midland House, West Way, Botley, Oxford, OX2 0PH
443 Park Avenue South, New York, NY, 10016, USA
E-mail; info@ospreypublishing.com

© 2007 Osprey Publishing Limited

ISBN 13: 978 1 84603 202 8

Edited by Tony Holmes
Page design by Tony Truscott
Cover Artwork by Mark Postlethwaite
Aircraft Profiles by Chris Davey
Index by Alan Thatcher
Printed in China

07 08 09 10 11   10 9 8 7 6 5 4 3 2 1

For a catalogue of all books published by Osprey please contact:

NORTH AMERICA
Osprey Direct, C/o Random House Distribution Center,
400 Hahn Road, Westminster, MD 21157
E-mail:info@ospreydirect.com

ALL OTHER REGIONS
Osprey Direct UK, PO Box 140 Wellingborough, Northants, NN8 2FA, UK
E-mail: info@ospreydirect.co.uk
www.ospreypublishing.com

CONTENTS

IN THE *LAFAYETTE* TRADITION

Although the United States did not enter World War 2 until December 1941, by then a significant number of American citizens had seen action in the British cause as fighter pilots serving with the Royal Air Force. These men were following in a tradition of foreign service established during World War 1 when, from 1915, American volunteers that had enlisted in the French army began transferring to the French air service. Eventually, in April of the following year, the French agreed to the formation of a unit composed of American pilots, and so the *Escadrille Americaine* – officially known as N124 – was formed. However, because of German objections since the USA was still neutral, in December 1916 it was renamed the *Escadrille Lafayette*.

With the unit's growing success came increased fame, resulting in a flow of American volunteers seeking service with N124, although applicants did not always serve with this *Escadrille*. Nevertheless, all these men passed through the Lafayette Flying Corps, which was a body established to assist Americans seeking service with the French air service.

The *Escadrille Lafayette* had been credited with 41 confirmed victories by the time it was transferred to the US Air Service in February 1918.

When Britain again went to war with Germany in September 1939, a number of adventurous young Americans – some of them experienced pilots – volunteered their services, often travelling to the UK via Canada, while others were recruited in the USA. Some saw action over France and England in the spring of 1940, while the first American pilots to fly the Spitfire began their training with No 7 Operational Training Unit in early July, just as the Battle of Britain began.

The six Americans that flew Spitfires in this epic campaign were Plt Offs 'Art' Donahue (No 64 Sqn), Hugh Reilley (No 66 Sqn), 'Red' Tobin, 'Shorty' Keough and Andrew Mamedorf (all with No 609 Sqn) and Phil Leckrone (No 616 Sqn). The triumvirate of Americans sent to No 609 Sqn joined the unit at Middle Wallop on 5 August, and were described by one of the British officers as 'typical Americans – amusing, always ready with some devastating wisecrack, and altogether excellent company. Our three Yanks became a quite outstanding feature of the squadron'.

'Art' Donahue became the first American to see combat in a Spitfire when, on the day his compatriots joined No 609 Sqn, he flew a patrol over the coast near Dover in K9991. He wrote afterwards, 'My pulses pounded and my thoughts raced'. His inexperience was soon revealed, for his Spitfire quickly ended up with a pair of Bf 109Es on its tail and was hit. 'It shook the aeroplane and was followed by a noise like hail on a tin roof', Donahue recounted. He managed to get down safely at Hawkinge, although his aircraft was badly damaged. During an action over convoy *Peewit* on the 8th, however, he became the first American to make a claim

The first confirmed victory by an American flying a Spitfire was claimed by Plt Off 'Red' Tobin of No 609 Sqn, who, during an attack on London on 15 September 1940, was credited with sharing in the destruction of a Do 17 (*JSCSC*)

Tobin's victim on 15 September is thought to have been this Do 17Z (F1+FS of 8./KG 76), flown by Fw R Heitsch, which crash-landed on the side of a hill near the village of Shoreham, in Kent (*via C H Goss*)

in a Spitfire when he damaged a Bf 109E, but on the afternoon of the 12th he baled out of X4018 wounded by burns and shrapnel after a fight with more Emils. Following four weeks in hospital recuperating, Donahue rejoined No 64 Sqn, before moving to Spitfire-equipped No 91 Sqn, with whom he eventually made five claims.

No 609 Sqn's American trio flew their first operational sorties on 16 August, but in his first action over Southampton eight days later (on his 28th birthday), Andy Mamedorf, who was in L1082/PR-A, soon found a Bf 109E behind him. A cannon shell hit the Spitfire's tail, smashed through the fuselage and buried itself in the pilot's back armour, yet Mamedorf still managed to fly the heavily damaged fighter back to base. Late the following afternoon, in a fight with Bf 110s off the Isle of Wight, 'Red' Tobin hit and damaged two fighter destroyers. Having forgotten to turn on his oxygen prior to engaging the enemy, he passed out moments later, however, and did not recover until just 1000 ft above the waves!

Mamedorf's next claim came on what is now commemorated as Battle of Britain Day, 15 September. Whilst defending London, No 609 Sqn claimed a number of Do 17s destroyed, with Tobin being credited with sharing in the destruction of one of them, thought to have been F1+FS of 8./KG 76, which crash-landed near Shoreham, in Kent. Tobin recorded in his diary, 'I caught a Dornier, chased him, shot his aileron off and hit his glycol tank. He went into cloud. I went down after him and saw it make a crash-landing. Crew of three got out'. This is thought to have been the first enemy aircraft destroyed by an American in a Spitfire.

US pilots in the other squadrons had, by then, also been introduced to operations, 'Zeke' Leckrone having joined No 616 Sqn at Coltishall on 2 September. Two weeks later he scrambled with his section after a 'plot' that turned out to be a Ju 88 which, after a long chase, they claimed as damaged. The aircraft, from 4(F)./122, in fact failed to return. Of the

The first American pilot to be killed in action in a Spitfire was Plt Off Hugh Reilley of No 66 Sqn, who was shot down by Maj Werner Molders, then the Luftwaffe's leading *experte*, on 17 October 1940 (*Classic Publications*)

Reilley was killed whilst flying Spitfire I R6800/LZ-N of No 66 Sqn, which is seen here running up at Gravesend a short time before its destruction (*No 66 Sqn Records*)

other Americans, Hugh Reilley from Detroit joined No 66 Sqn on the day Tobin claimed his victory, but on a patrol during the afternoon of 17 October, when flying R6800/LZ-N, he had the misfortune to meet Bf 109Es from JG 51 over Westerham and was shot down and killed by the unit's *Geschwaderkommodore*, and leading ace, Maj Werner Molders.

FIRST ACE

In the autumn of 1940, the RAF, for a variety of reasons, decided to group the volunteer American pilots into their own distinctive squadron along the lines of the *Escadrille Lafayette*. So, on 19 September, No 71 Sqn was formed as the first 'Eagle' squadron, and amongst those pilots posted to the unit was Phil Leckrone and No 609 Sqn's trio of 'Yanks'. The new unit was initially equipped with a handful of highly unsuitable US-built Brewster Buffalo fighters, although these were replaced with Hurricanes. The unit became operational in February 1941, and two further 'Eagle' squadrons – Nos 121 and 133 – were formed, again with Hurricanes.

Although these units made a series of claims for aircraft downed during sweeps over France, the increasing numbers of eager Americans arriving in the UK wanted to fly Spitfires – and pressure to re-equip the 'Eagle' squadrons mounted. So, in early August 1941, No 71 Sqn received a full complement of well-used Spitfire IIs, pending receipt of the latest Mk Vs. At least the Americans now had 'Spits'. They flew their first 'Circus' (bomber escort) mission on 27 August when the unit formed part of the escort for Blenheim bombers sent to attack the steel works at Lille.

Flying Spitfire IIA P7308/XR-D on this mission was Plt Off Bill Dunn, who had been one of the first 'Eagles' to make a claim on 2 July, and who by now had three victories flying Hurricanes. The Luftwaffe was tempted up to engage the Blenheims, and Dunn described the action that took place over Ambleteuse at 0820 hrs in his combat report;

'I dived on one of two Me 109Fs, fired from a distance of 150 yards, and fired again to within 50 yards. Pieces of the aircraft flew off and engine oil spattered my windscreen. The aeroplane looked like a blow-torch, with a bluish white flame as it went down. Tracers from another Me 109F behind me flashed past my cockpit. I pulled back the throttle, jammed down the flaps and skidded my aeroplane sharply out of his gun sight. The German overshot me by about ten feet, and as he crossed over-head, I could see the black insignia, unit markings and a red rooster painted on the side of the cockpit.

The first American to be credited with five victories in World War 2 was Plt Off Bill Dunn, who achieved this distinction when claiming No 71 Sqn's first Spitfire kills on 27 August 1941 (*via Norman Franks*)

'The Me 109F was now in my range. With a burst of only three seconds, I had put him out of commission. A wisp of smoke from the engine turned into a sheet of flame. The aeroplane rolled over on its back. As it started down, the tail section broke off. I had claimed my second victim of the day.'

However, Dunn's triumph was short lived, as moments later a burst of fire hit the cockpit of his Spitfire, turning his right leg into a bloodied mess, and he spun away barely conscious. Coming to, and in great pain, he made a slow descent towards the English coast, some 50 miles away – Dunn's escape was made more difficult through damage to the rear fuselage and rudder controls of his Spitfire. Escorted by two other aircraft, he successfully landed at Hawkinge, from where Dunn was rushed off to hospital with much of his right foot missing.

Seriously wounded, Bill Dunn was treated in the Royal Victoria hospital in Folkestone, and then spent three months recuperating. He had, nonetheless, become the first American pilot of World War 2 to be credited with five confirmed victories, and the first of no fewer than 69 American aces who achieved at least part of their total flying the Spitfire.

Despite having been badly wounded during his history-making engagement on 27 August 1941, Bill Dunn managed to get battle-damaged Spitfire IIA P7308/XR-D back to Hawkinge, from where he was rushed off to hospital. Seen here parked in the dispersal area at the Kent coast base, the fighter's scars of battle are readily visible on its rear fuselage (*RAF Hawkinge*)

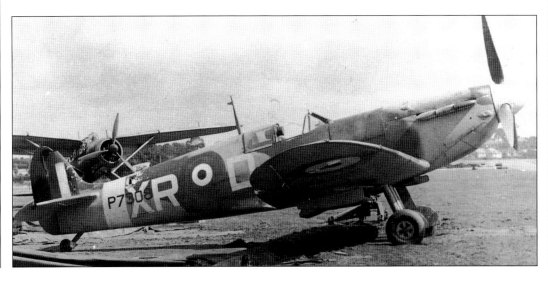

'EAGLES' OVER ENGLAND

As the original 'Eagle' squadron was beginning to flex its muscles on operations, in May 1941 the second unit, No 121 Sqn, was formed, followed by the third, and last, No 133 Sqn, in August, just as No 71 Sqn began receiving Spitfires. The latter unit flew its first Spitfire patrols from North Weald on the 17th, with Plt Offs 'Gus' Daymond and Chesley Peterson amongst the pilots involved. From 20 August all operations flown by No 71 Sqn were exclusively Spitfire affairs, although the Mk IIs flown by the unit were only on strength for a matter of weeks. Indeed, Bill Dunn's two victories described in the previous chapter were the only ones claimed with these aircraft. By month-end the first cannon-armed Spitfire VBs had arrived at North Weald for No 71 Sqn.

These aircraft were soon in action on cross-Channel sweeps, and near Mazingarbe on 4 September, Daymond, who already had three victories to his credit flying Hurricanes, shot down a Bf 109F. Three days later, in the late afternoon, unit CO Sqn Ldr Stanley Meares led a dozen of No 71 Sqn's Spitfires on a sweep that was engaged by three times as many Bf 109s. In heavy fighting near Boulogne, 'Pete' Peterson claimed his first victory, but three aircraft, including that of 'Red' Tobin, were lost – another of the original 'Eagles' had gone.

Such missions involving the American unit drew much press attention, and when, on the 19th, the modest 'Gus' Daymond shot down another Bf 109 off Dunkirk to claim his fifth victory, he was the object of considerable publicity. The Eagles had 'arrived', at least in the eyes of the British and American public. No 71 Sqn continued to find regular action on offensive sorties over the Continent, and two days later another American began his path to 'acedom' when Plt Off 'Red' McColpin, who, at 27, was one of the older 'Eagles', shot down a Bf 109E to the west of Lille.

To help his pilots gain operational experience, and taking advantage of clearing weather following days of low cloud, Sqn Ldr Meares led some of the newcomers on a patrol over the English Channel on 2 October. Flying as his wingman in AB908/XR-Y was McColpin. At 1340 hrs the latter spotted a group of about 20 Messerschmitt fighters a few hundred feet below, and having reported them, followed Meares as

Two of No 71 Sqn's leading pilots were Flg Off Gus Daymond (left) and Flt Lt Chesley Peterson, who both became aces and later transferred to the USAAF's 4th FG (*ww2images*)

he dived to attack. Meares fired on the nearest Bf 109, with his new wingman following up with a half-second burst from less than 50 yards, which caused the enemy fighter to burst into flames. McColpin later reported;

'I broke away to port and found myself in position for an attack on another Me-109, so I gave him a burst. He pulled up and dived with smoke pouring out. I thought I saw the pilot bale out. The aeroplane was seen to hit the ground. I saw another Me-109 below, dived on him, and followed him down to 3000 ft, where I gave him a one-second burst. He never pulled out, and he hit the deck as I pulled up.'

No 71 Sqn was credited with five destroyed following this clash, and three days later the King presented the unit's first DFCs to Daymond and Peterson.

However, in spite of a steady flow of success, casualties also mounted. On 20 October Peterson led newcomer Plt Off Oscar Coen (a schoolteacher from North Dakota) on a *Rhubarb*. Peterson described Coen as 'a real crackerjack, who had pretty well "graduated"'. That day they attacked a freight train near Lille, and during one of the strafing passes debris damaged the glycol system in Coen's Spitfire and he was forced to bale out. Evading capture, he managed to escape via Spain following many adventures and eventually rejoined the squadron soon after Christmas.

A few days prior to Coen's loss, on yet another *Rhubarb*, 'Red' McColpin surprised an Hs 126 observation/communications aircraft near Etaples and shot it down, before proceeding to strafe a train. Then, on 27 October, he shot down a pair of Bf 109s just south of Dunkirk, and so became the third 'Eagle' ace. More significantly in the context of this volume, McColpin was the first American ace to make all his claims in Spitfires. He too was awarded a DFC soon afterwards.

Offensive sorties over France resulted in a steady stream of casualties. One was Plt Off M W Fessler of No 71 Sqn, whose Spitfire VB (AA855/XR-C) was hit by debris from a train that he was attacking on 27 October 1941. The pilot was left with little choice but to force-land in a nearby field and become a PoW (*author's collection*)

On the day that Fessler was lost, Flt Lt 'Red' McColpin became the first American pilot to 'make ace' having claimed all his victories flying the Spitfire. He is seen here (second from right) being congratulated on his feat, and the award of the DFC, in front of his Spitfire VB AB908/XR-Y (*Classic Publications*)

—SPITFIRES FOR ALL!—

It was a sign of the growing maturity of the 'Eagle' squadrons that when Sqn Ldr Stanley Meares was killed in a mid air collision on 15 November, his place was taken by 21-year-old Chesley Peterson. One of his RAF flight commanders was nine-victory ace Flt Lt Royce Wilkinson, who said of him, 'Peterson was a

very good lad, level headed and mature, who spent much time studying flying, fighting and command'.

During the autumn of 1941, much to their delight, both of the remaining 'Eagle' squadrons also began re-equipping with the Spitfire. Initially, No 121 Sqn received Mk IIAs, but in November cannon-armed Mk VBs arrived at the unit's Kirton-in-Lindsey base. Much more to the squadron's liking, these aircraft were soon in action when, on 15 November, No 121 Sqn downed its first aircraft with the new fighters. Sadly, in a case of mistaken identity, this first 'success' proved to be a Blenheim rather than a Ju 88. The next day, however, Plt Off Hal Marting came across a genuine Junkers bomber whilst on a convoy patrol and succeeded in inflicting damage on the aircraft before it escaped.

On 28 October, Eglinton-based No 133 Sqn received its first Spitfire IIs, but retained some Hurricane IIs until early 1942, when, on moving to Kirton-in-Lindsey, it received Spitfire VBs. British five-victory ace Sqn Ldr Eric Thomas was posted in as CO of No 133 Sqn at this time, and 'Red' McColpin also arrived to take up the role of flight commander.

By no means all Americans joined the 'Eagle' squadrons, however, with many enrolling in the Royal Canadian Air Force (RCAF) and serving with its units once in the UK. One such individual was Plt Off Don Blakeslee, who had joined No 401 Sqn at Biggin Hill in May 1941. Eventually becoming one of the most influential American fighter leaders of the war, Blakeslee opened his combat account when he tangled with Bf 109s just before lunch on 18 November when flying Spitfire VB AD421/YO-H over the sea west of Le Touquet. No 401 Sqn's war diary described how he, 'fired a short burst and broke away immediately. He did not notice the result, but Plt Off Gilbert, coming in behind, noticed pieces flying from the aircraft'. Blakeslee was credited with a 'damaged'.

During a late afternoon sweep over the French coast south of Calais four days later, his unit, and No 72 Sqn, ran into a large number of enemy fighters. Blakeslee made a stern attack on the leading Bf 109 in a section of four, causing an explosion in its centre section. It was last seen trailing flames and thick black smoke as it went down out of control. Then, over

In October 1941, No 121 Sqn (the second 'Eagle' unit) began re-equipping with Spitfires – initially the Mk IIA, such as P8136/AV-S seen here during an anti-gas exercise (*Z Hurt*)

the coast upon returning to England, he spotted two more Bf 109s and attacked the No 2 aircraft, causing pieces to fly off as his fire struck aft of the cockpit. He was credited with one destroyed and a damaged.

Another American to enjoy success with the RCAF was Plt Off Jim Goodson, who flew with No 416 Sqn in 1942. He said of the Spitfire, 'The first time I got onto the tail of an enemy aeroplane in a Spitfire, I missed him. It wasn't because I opened fire before I was in range, or

anything like that. I should have blown him to bits, but the firing button was on top of the control column, and the Spitfire was so sensitive that, when I pressed the trigger, the nose pitched down and I missed the target. When you got used to the Spit you became part of it. You didn't aim your guns – you aimed yourself'.

With the coming of winter, many 'Circus' operations were curtailed, so the squadrons flew occasional 'Rhubarbs' (freelance fighter-only sweeps) instead, and losses mounted. During one on 7 December 1941, Plt Off R F Patterson was killed near Blankenberge, in Belgium – No 121 Sqn's first combat loss. The unit's wish for more sustained action finally happened when, on the 16th, it moved to North Weald to replace No 71 Sqn, thus becoming part of No 11 Group, in the very heart of Fighter Command's frontline. No 71 Sqn, in turn, moved north to Martlesham Heath, in Norfolk, from where it too continued operations.

Now based at Kirton-in-Lindsey, No 133 Sqn finally claimed its first victory on 5 February 1942, when, in spite of thick snow, a patrol took off into the overcast Lincolnshire skies, as the unit's record book described;

'The real fun began in the afternoon between 1500 and 1530 hrs when Flt Lt Johnston, with Plt Off Jackson as his No 2, and Flt Lt McColpin, with Sgt Wicker, were on a patrol over a coastal convoy. Flt Lt Johnston and Plt Off Jackson had combats with Do 217s that were trying to bomb the convoy – it was confirmed at 1530 hrs that a Do 217 was seen to definitely crash into the sea.

'McColpin had even more fun over the ships. No sooner did he arrive than he began a more or less uninterrupted series of actions with one or more Dorniers, lasting 15 minutes. He knocked out the gunner in one bomber, then shot pieces off one engine of the same Dornier.'

McColpin was credited with a damaged.

Soon afterwards, during the audacious 'Channel Dash' by a German naval squadron, including the battlecruisers *Scharnhorst* and

Arguably the most influential American fighter leader in the ETO was Don Blakeslee, who began his combat career flying Spitfires with No 401 Sqn RCAF. His initial claims were made at the controls of Mk VB BL753/YO-H, which he is seen climbing out of at Gravesend in May 1942 (*Classic Publications*)

Plt Off Jim Goodson (right) was another successful American who began his career with the RCAF, flying Spitfires with No 416 Sqn in 1942. On the left is Canadian Plt Off Jackie Rae, who claimed 2 and 2 shared victories and 3 damaged with No 416 Sqn in 1942-43 (*J Goodson via Norman Franks*)

One of the colourful characters that flew with the 'Eagles' was Plt Off Leo Nomis of No 71 Sqn, who recalled his ancestry by marking his aircraft with an Indian chief's head (*Leo Nomis*)

The most successful American pilot to fly the Spitfire was Plt Off John Lynch, who served with No 71 Sqn following brief spells with Nos 232 and 121 Sqns. He is seen here examining the damaged wing of his Spitfire after hitting a telegraph pole near Boulogne during a strafing attack (*JSCSC*)

Gneisenau and the heavy cruiser *Prinz Eugen* on 14 February, No 121 Sqn sent off four Spitfires in dreadful weather, but to little avail.

On 8 March, the unit provided 12 Spitfires as close escort for Bostons of Nos 88 and 226 Sqns sent to attack Commines power station. Future ace Plt Off Jim Daley, in Spitfire VB AD139, duly damaged an Fw 190 south of Dunkirk for his first claim. However, Plt Off 'Casey' Jones was lost, as was North Weald Wing Leader, and ten-kill ace, Wg Cdr Tony Eyre (flying No 121 Sqn Spitfire VB BL661). Both men became PoWs.

In spite of the unit's sustained efforts in combat, No 121 Sqn was still without a confirmed victory, but its luck finally changed on the afternoon of 23 March, when, during a sweep with Nos 222 and 403 Sqns, Sgt Jack Mooney downed an Fw 190 near Calais for the first of his three kills. The following day future American ace Plt Off Reade Tilley made his first claim by probably destroying an Fw 190 off Cap Griz Nez. He left No 122 Sqn soon afterwards and joined No 601 Sqn, which was then posted to Malta.

No 71 Sqn had also remained in action through the spring of 1942, and during this period the pilot destined to become the most successful American Spitfire ace of them all opened his account on 17 April. Plt Off John Lynch shared in the destruction of a Ju 88 with Plt Off Leo Nomis, who described the event many years later;

'By April I had acquired a personal Spitfire – BL287 XR-C – which I rather adolescently adorned with a Red Indian head to signify that I was, to a certain degree, of Sioux Indian ancestry.

'On 17 April I was involved in the interception of a Ju 88 which had made a hit-and-run attack on a convoy east of the Suffolk port of Felixstowe. My companion, J J Lynch, attacked from dead astern. I saw black smoke coming out of Lynch's engine and he pulled away to port, saying on the R/T that he had been hit. Again I closed in, firing, until the bomber reared on its tail, hung quivering for a moment, then dived straight into the sea. My own aircraft was hit, but I managed to return to Martlesham Heath with an almost empty fuel tank.'

In spite of his Spitfire being seriously damaged, John Lynch limped back to the Suffolk coast, where he crash-landed, suffering injuries to his face.

A week later No 121 Sqn's Plt Off Jim Daley also claimed his first confirmed kill when returning from a sweep, the action being colourfully described at the time in the following entry from the unit's record book. 'Plt Offs Daley and Skinner saw a Ju 52 and jointly attacked it. The result of these attacks were clouds of white smoke, and bits were seen to fly off the enemy aircraft. Quickly after this it was seen to fall into the sea with a great splash'. Their victim was, in fact, a rather elderly Ju 34W.

No 71 Sqn's American CO, Sqn Ldr Chesley Peterson, was also steadily accumulating victories, and combat experience, during the spring of 1942. On 27 April he destroyed two Fw 190s near St Omer, while the prodigal Oscar Coen shared in the destruction of three more Focke-Wulf fighters.

No 133 Sqn finally moved south to Biggin Hill from Kirton-in-Lindsey in early May to add its weight to the RAF's broadening offensive over France. Its first success following the move came near Abbeville on the 17th, as its Operational Record Book (ORB) relates;

'The squadron succeeded in stirring up the Hun's nest! Flt Lt McColpin and Plt Off Morris both had combats five miles northwest of Le Treport, as a result of which McColpin claimed an ME 109F destroyed and another as a "probable". Neither they nor any of the remaining pilots suffered any damage.'

These would in fact prove to be 'Red' McColpin's final claims with the RAF, taking his total to eight destroyed, although he would later make three further victory claims in August 1944 whilst flying P-47Ds with the USAAF's 404th FG.

No 121 Sqn was also up on 17 May, and near St Omer Flg Off 'Sel' Edner attacked an Fw 190, which exploded for his second victory, and Daley shot another down in flames. The squadron also flew some 'Roadsteads' (shipping reconnaissance missions) during this period, with future ace Flt Lt

The third 'Eagle' squadron was No 133, which was led by RAF ace Sqn Ldr Eric Thomas. His personal aircraft was BM263/MD-A, seen here, which he used to claim one victory, one probable and two damaged between May and October 1942. It carried a personal marking and the title *MILD & BITTER* beneath the cockpit. Also note the RAF roundel on the wheel hub (*Stars & Stripes via J D R Rawlings*)

One of the 'Eagles' who developed into a much-respected leader was No 121 Sqn's Plt Off Jim Daley, who is seen here at Kirton-in-Lindsey on 27 November 1941. He became a squadron commander upon transferring to the USAAF (*Classic Publications*)

Barry Mahon describing just such a sortie on 20 May;

'We lined up astern and made passes, one after another, at an armed trawler. The trawler returned our fire until our bullets and shells wiped out the resistance. Those of us coming in last were able to blow a gaping hole in the side with our cannon, and the ship sank.'

A week later Flg Off Jim Daley blew up a minesweeper and Mahon and two other pilots destroyed another. As the Spitfires pulled away, they were attacked by eight Bf 109Fs, and Daley, flying BL986, shot one down.

The action also remained intense for No 133 Sqn, as future ace Flt Sgt 'Dixie' Alexander wrote following a sortie on the 29th;

'I fired at an enemy aircraft for the first time today. It was an Me 109, which flew past and below my section. Sqn Leader Thomas had just fired on a Fw 190, and we were on our way down after him, when this aircraft passed below, giving me almost a full deflection opportunity.'

Alexander had also recently been allocated his own aircraft in the form of Spitfire VB BM353/MD-I.

Flg Off Daley was awarded a DFC on 1 June, and that same day Chesley Peterson led No 71 Sqn when it provided part of an escort force for Hurricanes conducting a 'Circus' to Bruges. A formation of Fw 190s from I. and II./JG 26, led by Maj Gerhard Schopfel, were spotted, and as they egressed near Blankenburgh, the intruders were soon heavily engaged. Peterson quickly led White Section after a dozen German fighters, and pulling hard, and with his throttle closed, he managed to get behind a Focke-Wulf at a range of only 100 yards and fire off two bursts, which struck the fighter's wing root and cockpit and sent it spinning away trailing smoke.

Climbing back up to 20,000 ft, Peterson then spotted the Spitfires of No 350 Sqn, which were also under attack. Moments later, he too was bounced by Fw 190s, although he managed to disengage and head for home, having claimed his coveted fifth victory. Red Section, led by Flt Lt 'Gus' Daymond, also scrapped with the Fw 190s, and the ace soon found himself in a tight turning fight with five German fighters. He too managed to shake off his foes and return home, but not before he had claimed his sixth success. Daymond landed at Manston with just 2½ gallons of fuel remaining in the tanks of his Spitfire!

Enter the USAAF

The United States entered World War 2 in the wake of the 7 December 1941 attack on Pearl Harbor by the Japanese. In mid-1942, the newly created Eighth Air Force began establishing itself in England, with its 31st Fighter Group (FG) arriving at Atcham and High Ercall, in Shropshire, in late June. There, the group received Spitfires under a reverse lend-lease arrangement, as its P-39s were deemed to be unsuitable for the fighter role in Europe. Group CO was Col John Hawkins, and his three squadron commanders were Maj Marvin McNickle (307th FS), Maj Fred Dean (308th) and Maj Harrison Thyng (309th), the latter being a future ace.

The 52nd FG, comprising the 2nd, 4th and 5th FSs, also sailed for Britain at around this time too, and upon its arrival at Eglinton, in Northern Ireland, these units also received Spitfires, much to the delight of their pilots. The 52nd's Executive Officer (XO), Maj James Coward, commented at the time;

'The Spit is an easy aeroplane to fly, but the braking system and distribution of weight in the nose has caused us a little trouble. The British are to be commended for the excellent job they did of training both air and ground personnel.'

For the hard-pressed RAF, the arrival of six more fighter squadrons was also no doubt welcome. Both the American groups were to fly the British fighter with distinction, with a large number of pilots achieving ace status in the Spitfire.

While the fledgling USAAF units worked up, it was business as usual for the 'Eagle' squadrons, and during a 'Rodeo' (a pre-planned fighter-only sweep) in the first week of June, Flt Lts Mahon and Mooney each shot down two Fw 190s, but on the 16th the latter was added to the increasing list of American 'Eagle' casualties when he was killed near Ostend during a 'Rhubarb'. By the time of his death Mooney had made a total of five claims, including three destroyed. A month later, on 19 July, Plt Offs Johnnie Lynch and Helgason flew a 'Rhubarb' in poor weather. Near Nieuport, a pair of Fw 190s broke cloud and came at them head on.

One of the early Spitfires used by the USAAF's 309th FS whilst undergoing type conversion training at High Ercall was Mk VB BM635/WZ-Y, which was flown by future ace 2Lt Dale Shafer in late June 1942 (*Harry Holmes*)

Lynch fired at one as it closed and flashed by, the Fw 190 half-rolling onto its back. Lynch then spotted others just beneath the cloud, and he fired on these too, before pulling up into the cloud to take cover. Another pilot had seen his first Focke-Wulf go into the sea.

As part of the working up of the USAAF, six senior pilots from the 31st FG were attached to RAF units to gain operational experience flying cross-Channel sorties. The first was conducted on 26 July, when three pilots flew a sweep with No 412 Sqn RCAF. Unfortunately, 31st FG XO Lt Col Albert P Clark was shot down over France and became a PoW – he thus became the first USAAF fighter casualty in the European theatre.

Gradually, by early August, all the squadrons from both USAAF groups were declared operational and available for combat operations, initially for defensive patrols and some convoy escorts. Later, they participated as escorts for US bombing raids on targets in northern France. To further expose their pilots to operational conditions, the 2nd and 4th FSs from the 52nd FG moved into the frontline at Biggin Hill and Kenley, respectively, while 31st FG squadrons were also posted to bases in the southeast. Amongst the latter was the 309th FS, which was sent to Westhampnett.

During a practice gunnery flight on 8 August, a flight from this unit was vectored after some Fw 190s over nearby Shoreham that had just conducted a nuisance raid. Maj Thyng spotted one of the German fighters, and after an exciting chase, he opened fire and claimed it damaged – the USAAF's first fighter claim in Europe. Harry Thyng later became an ace flying Spitfires in the MTO.

The 'Eagles', too, continued to be active, with No 121 Sqn having the most successful day of its existence on 31 July when it escorted Bostons returning from an attack on Abbeville airfield. Patrolling off the coast near Berck-sur-Mer, No 121 Sqn became engaged in a tremendous fight. Its CO, Sqn Ldr Hugh Kennard, destroyed a Bf 109F, as did Sgt Kelly, whilst Flt Lt Edner downed two more Messerschmitt fighters and Plt Off Barry Mahon two Fw 190s. One Spitfire was lost and the CO was wounded, being fortunate to coax his Spitfire back to a crash-landing at Lympne. He was replaced by six-kill ace Sqn Ldr W D Williams, who led the unit for the first time on 3 August.

Later that month No 121 Sqn's pilots escorted their countrymen of the Eighth Air Force for the first time when, on the 17th, they took the 340th Bomb Squadron on a feint attack to cover the first B-17

To gain operational experience, some 31st FG pilots initially flew under the auspices of No 412 Sqn RCAF. Unfortunately, during their first sortie on 26 July 1942, the group's Executive Officer, Lt Col Albert Clark, was shot down by Fw 190s while flying Spitfire VB BL964/VZ-G and captured – he thus became the first USAAF fighter pilot to be lost in action in the ETO (*via Wojtek Matusiak*)

On 8 August 1942, Maj Harrison R Thyng, CO of the 309th FS, damaged an Fw 190 off Shoreham. This success gave him the distinction of being the first USAAF Spitfire pilot to make a claim in the ETO. Thyng duly 'made ace' in the Spitfire in the Mediterranean during 1943 (*via Jerry Scutts*)

raid on France. Also part of the escort was No 401 Sqn, one of whose pilots was future six-victory ace Flt Sgt Eddie Gimbel from Chicago, who opened his account by probably destroying an Fw 190 – he shared another probable too. The following day, Flt Lt Don Blakeslee, who, somewhat reluctantly, had recently transferred to No 133 Sqn, claimed his second victory when he shot down an Fw 190 of 2./JG 26, flown by Ltn Rahardt.

DIEPPE BATTLE

The first taste of real action for the USAAF Spitfire groups came on 19 August, when the 31st FG formed part of the fighter cover for the large-scale raid on the French port of Dieppe, which was to see some of the heaviest air fighting of the war. In company with Nos 130 and 131 Sqns of the RAF, a dozen Spitfires of the 309th FS left Westhampnett early for Dieppe. Over the beachhead, they were attacked by a swarm of Fw 190s, and in the ensuing dogfight Lt Samuel F Junkin Jr managed to shoot one down to claim the first fighter victory for the USAAF in Europe. However, moments later he was attacked and wounded by a second Focke-Wulf and forced to bale out – Junkin was rescued by a torpedo boat that also picked up squadronmate Lt Collins.

Future ace Flt Sgt Ed Gimbel, who flew with No 401 Sqn RCAF, made his first claims 48 hours before the ill-fated Dieppe raid. He is seen here relaxing prior to flying a sortie during Operation *Jubilee* (*Canadian Forces*)

Also over Dieppe that day in a 308th FS Spitfire was Capt Frank Hill, who, having left Kenley at around 0700 hrs, recalled;

'We arrived over the target area on time and split into four-ship formations. Patrolling the area, we were at an altitude of about 8000 to 10,000 ft. We soon received a report from ground control that 12+ enemy aircraft were heading our way, and they arrived shortly thereafter at about 12,000 ft. They immediately pressed home the attack, and a general dogfight resulted, with the Spitfires staying in sections of four and the Focke-Wulfs and Me 109s mostly staying in pairs.

'After about three minutes of trying to keep my section from being hit, I finally caught an Fw 190 and fired about a four-second burst of cannon and machine gun shells into it at about 300 yards at a 45-degree angle on his port side. He rolled and spun down, with the smoke coming out, and when I last saw him he was at about 2000 ft and still in a steep dive. The action was much too hot to take time to follow him all the way down.'

Credited with a probable, this proved to be the first claim for the future ace. Fellow aces Maj Harrison Thyng, CO of the 309th, and Lt John H White of the 307th also claimed probables. It had, however, been a difficult blooding, as the inexperienced 31st FG lost eight Spitfires, with others damaged, resulting in one pilot being killed, one missing and three made PoWs.

For some reason this Spitfire VB of the 308th FS, seen at Kenley in July 1942, is fitted with an early pattern 'blunt' spinner. It was flown at this time by future ace Capt Frank Hill, although it is not known if this is the aircraft he was flying when he made his first claim over Dieppe on 19 August 1942 (*ww2images*)

All three 'Eagle' squadrons had also seen much action over Dieppe. Having flown an uneventful first sortie, after refuelling, No 71 Sqn returned to the beachhead, by which time the Luftwaffe had reacted. The oldest 'Eagle' pilot in the squadron, Plt Off Harold 'Pappy' Strickland, recalled as they approached;

'We split into three columns of fours. Blue Section, in which I was fighting, was ordered to climb toward a formation of Focke-Wulf 190s. We went for them, twisting and turning like an angry snake, manoeuvring and counter-manoeuvring with the 190s. But we soon saw they didn't actually want to fight – they just wanted to draw us away from the west flank of our convoy, thus exposing our ships to the bombers who were hovering around, waiting for a chance to get over the convoy and drop their bombs.

'A Ju 88 did manage to get through our high cover and come in. Pete, our CO, who was leading White Section, immediately spoke over the R/T. "Hurry up! Get that 88". Right away, we saw Red Section begin firing at the bomber. And we saw White Section, with Pete in front, almost standing their Spitfires on their tails as they came in terrifically fast from below. We in Blue Section had given up playing tag with the Focke-Wulf 190s, and we too were trying to get within range, but finally we reluctantly gave up the chase with the Hun bomber, with smoke streaming from its engines and some 15 Spitfires on its tail.'

Peterson was credited with damaging the Ju 88 on this sortie. On the next mission, at 1415 hrs, he destroyed another Ju 88 over the convoy for his final claim in the Spitfire, but was then forced down himself, although he too was picked up.

No 121 Sqn flew four missions during the day, the first taking off at 0840 hrs to cover the landing force. They were soon engaged in a whirling dogfight, and 'Sel' Edner shot down an Fw 190, but on the debit side three Spitfires went down. One was being flown by Flt Lt Barry Mahon, who had shot down an Fw 190 to become an ace just prior to being forced to take to his parachute over the sea following an attack by another German fighter;

'I lay on my back in the dinghy and watched the tremendous air battle above me. It seemed like the entire engagement was taking place right over my head, with aircraft being shot down, parachutes coming out of the sky and explosions everywhere. It seemed like a giant Fourth of July display, only much more tragic.'

Sqn Ldr Williams then led No 121 Sqn back over the beaches in deteriorating weather around midday, with the unit's final sortie coming in the late afternoon when it helped cover the withdrawal of troops from Dieppe. By a strange irony, Mahon's award of the DFC was promulgated the next day, by which point he was a PoW.

Spitfire VB BM590/AV-R *Olga* cruises over East Anglia in August 1942. It was flown over Dieppe on 19 August by Plt Off Gilbert Halsey, who claimed an Fw 190 probable during the course of the mission. On 5 September Flt Sgt Fink shared a Ju 88 destroyed in it (*Alastair Goodrum*)

No 133 Sqn, too, was placed on readiness early on 19 August, but it was not until breakfast time that the unit was ordered to Dieppe, led by Flt Lt Don Blakeslee. He and Flt Sgt 'Dixie' Alexander duly claimed a probable Fw 190 each on that first mission. By mid-morning the unit was once again in the thick of the action, with Blakeslee damaging another Fw 190 and destroying a Do 217. Squadronmate, and future ace, Plt Off Don Gentile also enjoyed success on this sortie, as he subsequently described in a letter written in 1949;

'My first two victories were over Dieppe while flying with No 133 Sqn. The FW 190 which I got on this occasion had just finished shooting down one of our Spitfires when I jumped him. He immediately started to roll for the deck, and I followed him, clobbering the FW 190 at about 3000 ft, at which time he lazily rolled over and slowly hit the beach where the Commandos were coming ashore.

'After I had gotten the FW 190, a JU 88 started to dive-bomb the troops on the ground. I managed to get on his tail and started to clobber him too. The JU 88 jettisoned its bombs in the Channel and missed its target. I closed in and got one engine burning. The aircraft finally exploded and crashed inland. These were my first two victories.'

No 133 Sqn was ordered to conduct a further patrol soon after midday, 'Dixie' Alexander flying as 'Yellow 3' as part of this mission;

'Just before we reached the target, we were bounced by two 190s, which came down on Yellow Section. I called the break and we turned into them in good time. I was able to follow the second 190 down, and fired a couple of short bursts at him.'

The Fw 190 escaped, but whilst trying to find his squadronmates Alexander then saw some aircraft attacking the escort destroyer HMS *Berkley*, which was so badly damaged that it later had to be sunk by other Royal Navy vessels;

'It was then that I saw six Do 217s just as they were dropping their bombs on the convoy. I singled out one 217, and closed to about 300 yards. I fired bursts into him until my cannons were exhausted. I had observed numerous hits, and his port engine was smoking. By this time we were south of Dieppe and over land, and I continued to fire short bursts of 0.303 as he made a gentle turn, dropped down and crash-landed in a field some two or three miles south of the town.'

At just before 2000 hrs, Flt Lt Blakeslee led No 133 Sqn over the last of the convoys returning survivors from the Dieppe debacle, although little aerial activity was seen. The unit finally landed at Lympne shortly before 2100 hrs, thus bringing Operation *Jubilee* to a close.

TRANSFER OF THE 'EAGLES'

With the increasing build up of the Eighth Air Force in Britain, the RAF and USAAF came to the decision that all three 'Eagle' squadrons would transfer to their national command at the end of September 1942. Pilots were gradually attested into US service, and most transferred with the equivalent RAF rank – McColpin, Daymond and Daley became majors, but most were transferred as captains or lieutenants, while the NCO pilots were, in the main, commissioned. Chesley Peterson, however, was promoted to lieutenant colonel, his leadership qualities being recognised by those serving with him. One of the latter was 'Art' Roscoe, who wrote;

When the 'Eagle' squadrons joined the Eighth Air Force in September 1942, 22-year-old Chesley Peterson was transferred from the RAF to the USAAF as a lieutenant colonel and made XO of the 4th FG (*Classic Publications*)

Six-victory ace 2Lt Roy Evans opened his account whilst flying Spitfires with the 335th FS, downing a Fieseler Fi 156 near Furnes during a sortie over France on 21 November 1942 (*via H Holmes*)

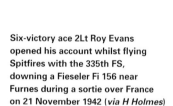

'He seemed to have an attitude about him that inspired confidence in the pilots. He was always calm, cool and collected, and seemed to know just what he was doing. Pete exemplified the right way of doing things, and doing your job properly. He was also a good pilot.'

On 5 September a section from No 121 Sqn found a marauding Ju 88, which was shot down into the sea east of the Naze for the unit's final kill. Shortly afterwards, one of the squadron's more successful pilots, 'Sel' Edner, was awarded the DFC for his fine work.

Concurrent with these changes, operations continued for all three units. Soon afterwards, Nos 71 and 121 Sqns moved to Debden, with No 133 Sqn going to its satellite airfield at Great Sampford.

The latter unit had just received some of the first improved Spitfire IXs to reach the frontline, and on the 26th a dozen of them had moved forward to Bolt Head, in Devon, from where they took off to support a 97th BG B-17 raid on Morlaix. Encountering much stronger tailwinds than had been forecast en route to the target, the fighters were pushed well beyond the point of no return, and low on fuel, 11 came down on the Brest Peninsula. Four pilots were killed, six taken prisoner and one managed to evade back to England.

No 133 Sqn's CO, Sqn Ldr 'Red' McColpin, had been ordered to report for transfer and attestation into the USAAF on the eve of this operation, and in spite of his protests, did not lead the mission, while Plt Off Don Gentile was only required as a spare, and thus did not fly.

Three days later, on 29 September, at a parade in the rain at Debden, the three 'Eagle' squadrons were formally transferred to the USAAF, respectively becoming the 334th, 335th and 336th FSs, led by Majs 'Gus' Daymond, Jim Daley and 'Red' McColpin. They formed the 4th FG, under Col E W Anderson, who had the highly regarded Lt Col Peterson as his deputy. Wg Cdr Myles Duke-Woolley, an experienced RAF commander with seven victories to his credit, temporarily held the post of Wing Leader. All three squadrons took with them into the USAAF much hard won battle experience and a proud record.

Whilst the Eighth Air Force had gained the 4th FG, it was in the process of losing the 31st and 52nd FGs, as having worked up to an

operational pitch, both groups had been earmarked for Operation *Torch* – the Anglo-American invasion of French North Africa. They were therefore taken off operations to prepare, under great secrecy, for this new venture. Both were transferred to Twelfth Air Force control and sent via sea to Gibraltar, the 31st sailing on 21 October and the 52nd two days later. The 31st, however, had a final fling, as on 22 September, during a press day at Westhampnett, a section from the 309th, led by Maj Thyng, was scrambled after an intruder. Thyng returned having probably destroyed a Ju 88.

For pilots flying with the 4th FG, initially little changed following the switch from the RAF to the USAAF other than their uniforms and the fact that their Spitfires now wore US 'star' roundels. Operations continued under RAF control, with the group making its first claims on 2 October during a 'Circus' when it was led by Wg Cdr Duke-Woolley. In a fight over the French coast between Calais and Dunkirk, four Fw 190s were confirmed destroyed, one of which Duke-Woolley shared with 2Lt Jim Clark, who duly made his first claim. Many years later, Duke-Woolley recalled the action;

'The weather wasn't awfully good on this day, and as we had not expected to fly, some of the chaps had pushed off to London. I took what pilots I had on base and soon we were floating around over France, when down below I suddenly saw a squadron of aircraft in a similar four-man section that we were now flying. I could see that they were 190s. I called the boys and told them to give me about 200 yards start, for I wanted the leader!

'My No 2 and I went down into the formation, and I got right above the three aircraft behind the leading 190, then arrived behind the leader – a matter of about ten yards. In fact I could look down to my left, right into the cockpit of one German just to the left of the leader. I knew perfectly well that at that

range I couldn't fire at him via the gun sight – I had to aim up a bit. I then gave him a two-second burst, then broke away, calling for the others to come down.

'I created a little confusion amongst the Germans, for I'd hit the leader absolutely dead right. I blew both wings off, which began to flutter down and then the fuselage nosed forward. The rest of the Germans just paused a moment then the other chaps were amongst them and we shot down three more, with some others damaged.'

The others were claimed by Gene Fetrow of the 335th and Stanley Anderson and Oscar Coen of the 334th.

By the end of the year the 4th FG had claimed nine enemy aircraft destroyed, but at a cost of 14 pilots. At the end of November McColpin returned to the USA and was replaced as CO of the 336th by Maj Don Blakeslee, while the formal RAF connection was finally severed in December when Duke-Woolley left and was replaced as Wing Leader by Peterson, who led the entire group for the first time on 4 January 1943.

As the only operational USAAF fighter unit in Europe, the 4th FG was subject to great attention by the rapacious American press, who naturally wanted to describe every action. They particularly wanted to report success whilst flying American aircraft, and so the 4th FG was earmarked to become an early recipient of the massive Republic P-47 Thunderbolt. Training on the new fighter began in mid January. The group's first success of 1943 came on 14 January when, just before midday off Ostend, Lts Stanley Anderson and Robert Boock each shot down an Fw 190. Eight days later this pair were also to be leading players in the last major combat involving Eighth Air Force Spitfires and the Luftwaffe.

At 1430 hrs on 22 January, Lt Col Peterson led the 335th and 336th FSs on a 'Circus' against St Omer airfield in company with some

Among the pilots that flew Spitfire VB EN783/XR-K of the 334th FS was 2Lt Steve Pisanos, who later became an ace with the squadron while flying P-47s and P-51s (*via J D Oughton*)

Spitfire VB BL766/MD-C of the 336th FS is seen at Debden in late 1942. This aircraft was often flown by Maj Don Blakeslee during his time as the squadron CO (*L Chick via R C B Ashworth*)

Bostons and the Spitfire-equipped Hornchurch Wing. As the second box of bombers, escorted by the 336th FS (with Oscar Coen as leader), left the area, they were followed by more than a dozen Fw 190s. Coen led the Spitfires in a climbing turn towards them, but the German fighters broke away. The Spitfires then swung back towards the bombers, at which point the Fw 190s attacked, as Coen vividly described;

'I was a few miles inside the French coast in a rather steep dive when I was attacked by four FW 190s. I turned with them about four turns, each time making for the coast, when they would get slung wide on the turn. I radioed Col Peterson for help and made for the coast again. One FW 190 pulled up below me and down sun, and began a climbing turn towards me from about 1000 yards. I turned towards him and then reversed my turn as he went in front of me, at which point I took a short beam shot and missed. My aircraft mushed down into a stern quarter turn as he climbed past me towards the sun. I gave him a short burst from about 150 yards, quarter astern, white smoke came out

Like his RAF equivalents, Lt Col Peterson identified his aircraft with his initials, part of which can just been seen under the cockpit of well-worn Spitfire VB BL449 at Debden in January 1943 (*L Chick via R C B Ashworth*)

Spitfire VB BL545/MD-L of the 336th FS was flown by Maj Oscar Coen during the 4th FG's last big fight prior to re-equipping with the P-47. The engagement took place near Dunkirk on 22 January 1943, and Coen downed an Fw 190 (*Eagle Association*)

Sitting in its revetment at Debden in February 1943 is Spitfire VB BM309/AV-V of the 335th FS. On 22 January it had been used by 2Lt Robert A Boock to destroy an Fw 190 northwest of Dunkirk in the 4th FG's last big engagement with the Spitfire (*D Young via R C B Ashworth*)

and he fell off on his port side and dived into the sea. The pilot did not bale out.'

This was Coen's fifth victory, thus making him the first of many Eighth Air Force aces. In a vicious fight, three more Fw 190s were claimed destroyed by the American Spitfires against one loss.

A few days before this, and much to the dismay of the older hands in the 4th FG, the group began converting to the Thunderbolt, but operations on Spitfires continued for a time. On 10 March Peterson led 14 of the 334th's P-47s on the type's first combat mission in the ETO, but this proved uneventful other than when the fighters' electrical system caused the radios to go berserk!

Former schoolteacher Maj Oscar Coen (right) had a colourful career with the 'Eagles', having been shot down and evaded capture to return to duty. He became a squadron commander on transferring to the USAAF, leading both the 334th and 336th FSs, and later in the war the 356th FG (*via Jerry Scutts*)

Two days later, 28 Spitfires from the 335th and 336th, led by Chesley Peterson, flew a sweep to the Dieppe area, but had no engagements. That same afternoon 23 aircraft from both squadrons performed another 'Rodeo' and crossed the French coast at Dunkirk. The 336th then headed towards Calais, and over Audruicq was attacked by a pair of Fw 190s. The 4th FG's final Spitfire claim was subsequently made moments later by one of its most distinguished pilots when 1Lt Don Gentile, flying Spitfire VB BL673, damaged a German fighter.

On 16 March 1943 the 4th FG's remaining Spitfires were officially taken off operations and stored in the 336th FS dispersal, although most of them continued to fly with the latter unit until the end of the month due to shortage of P-47s. The 4th FG, flying the Thunderbolt and later the Mustang, went on to become the most successful US fighter group in the ETO in terms of the number of aerial victories it claimed.

Although Spitfires no longer served as operational fighters with the USAAF in Britain, other Americans continued to fly them in the ETO, mainly with RCAF units. One such individual was newly commissioned Plt Off Eddie Gimbel, who on 17 January 1943 claimed his third victory. No 401 Sqn's war diary recounted how he 'saw two FW 190s above him. He got in a short attack on one, during which the enemy aircraft descended from 7000 ft to 3000 ft. He failed to see the FW 190 hit the deck, but its crash was observed by several other members of the squadron'.

A 4th FG legend, 1Lt Don Gentile of the 336th FS proudly stands in front of Spitfire VB BL255/MD-T, which not only featured his colourful nose art, but also his two victory symbols for his successes over Dieppe on 19 August 1942 (*via P Listemann*)

Gimbel left for No 403 Sqn soon afterwards, where he continued his success, shooting down another Fw 190 in late February. He claimed his fifth success, on 4 April, in somewhat unusual circumstances, as his Spitfire IX collided with an Fw 190 over central France in the area of Pouilly and he had to bale out. Picked up by the Resistance, Gimbel returned to the UK in early August. Now Flt Lt Gimbel, he made his final claim with No 421 Sqn during a dogfight between Merville and Douai on 20 December 1943 when he shot down an Fw 190. He transferred to the USAAF a few months later and served with the 4th FG, flying P-51s. Shot down by flak on 16 April 1945, Gimbel spent the last weeks of the war as a PoW.

The leading USAAF ace in Europe was Frank Gabreski, who, citing his Polish roots, initially gained operational experience flying Spitfires for a few weeks with No 315 'Polish' Sqn at Northolt (*via Wojtek Matusiak*)

Another American pilot to enjoy aerial success with the RCAF was New Yorker Sgt Jim Thorne, who joined No 402 Sqn at Merston during the summer of 1943. On the evening of 4 September, during a sweep between St Pol and Le Touquet, he shot down an Fw 190 to register his first victory. He made several more claims flying Spitfire VBs, the last of these coming on 22 April 1944 whilst at the controls of BL907 after he had moved to No

One of the aircraft flown on operations in January 1943 by Gabreski when attached to No 315 Sqn was Spitfire VB BS513/PK-Z (*via Wojtek Matusiak*)

504 Sqn when he shared in the destruction of a Ju 88 off the Orkneys in a rare engagement for that area. Thorne became an ace later that summer flying Mustangs with No 122 Sqn, and he was shot down and killed by flak on a reconnaissance mission over Velp, in Holland, on 10 September while still serving with this unit.

Finally, having last seen action in September 1942 when he was forced down over Sicily to become a PoW, 11-victory Malta ace Plt Off Claude Weaver returned from his incarceration to operations with No 403 Sqn, and on 30 December 1943 he shot down a Bf 109 southeast of Albert. Then, on 21 January 1944, Weaver downed an Fw 190 near Lens for his 13th success. However, one week later, on 28 January, during a four-aircraft 'Ranger' over France, his formation encountered a dozen Fw 190s. In the subsequent combat he was shot down and killed, almost certainly becoming the 18th victim of Fw Gerhard Vogt of 6./JG 26. Two months later Weaver's award of the DFC was promulgated.

With 12.5 aircraft destroyed and three probables, Claude Weaver was the second most successful American Spitfire pilot.

NORTH AFRICAN ADVENTURE

When the 31st and 52nd FGs had sailed from England, they left their Spitfire VBs behind, as new ones would be issued to the groups upon their arrival in Gibraltar. A handful of pilots from both groups had been flown to the 'Rock' to air test the Spitfires in preparation for their arrival. Much to his amazement, on landing in Gibraltar the advanced party's ranking officer, Maj Marvin McNickle of the 31st, was informed that he was now in charge of its air defence!

The *Torch* landings around Oran and Algiers began early on 8 November 1942, and the 31st FG's Spitfires headed for Oran from Gibraltar late that afternoon, led by group CO, Col John R Hawkins. Upon arriving over Tafaraoui, the CO landed, followed by Lt Byrd. However, as the latter pilot approached the runway, he was bounced by a Vichy French Dewoitine D.520 fighter and shot down and killed. This aircraft was one of four D.520s that had been misidentified as Hurricanes, and the remaining Spitfires promptly set off in pursuit of the fleeing fighters.

In the subsequent engagement, Maj Thyng and 1Lts Payne and Kenworthy each shot one down – these victories set both Thyng and Payne on the road to 'acedom'. In fact, they would be among only a handful of USAAF pilots to claim kills over German, Italian, Japanese and Vichy-French aircraft. Carl Payne recalled in his combat report;

'I had made my final turn with wheels and flaps down, and I heard over the radio that enemy aeroplanes were beating up our field. I immediately pulled up my flaps and wheels and started circling. I had made almost one complete circuit of the field when I saw three French Dewoitines diving upon the field with guns blazing. I then immediately attacked them, taking snap shots at them. I was then following two of the fighters. One of them broke away, and as he left, I gave him a good long deflection shot and saw no results.

'I then started climbing after the first Dewoitine, which was above me and out of my range. As I closed within range, I gave him a good three-second burst, seeing an explosive shell strike his wing. He half rolled and did an aileron turn downward – I followed, and he pulled up into a steep climb, or Immelman. I closed fast upon him, and at close range my machine guns peppered his fuselage and wings – I was out of cannon shells by this time. His right wing exploded and caught fire. The

The 308th FS initially saw little action over Algeria, but suffered occasional accidental losses, as happened to this Spitfire VC, which crash-landed at Maison Blanche on 12 December 1942 (*via Henry Boot*)

pilot baled out at 5000 ft. I watched both he and his aeroplane go down. The air was clear of enemy fighters by then, and we landed unmolested.'

The 52nd FG's squadrons flew into Oran over the next two days, settling at La Senia, which boasted only the most basic facilities. Because of bad weather en route, a few Spitfires landed in Spanish Morocco, where they were temporarily interned.

The RAF had also flown in several experienced fighter wings, and at the end of the month the 2nd FS was attached to No 322 Wing and sent east to Bone, from where it began flying sweeps and bomber escorts, as well as local defensive patrols. On 30 November, during a sweep over Teboura, the squadron claimed the 52nd FG's first victories, when Maj James Coward and Lt Warren each destroyed a Bf 109G. Coward, who later commanded the 52nd FG, reported;

'We were put on to two Me 109Gs by ground radio. We spotted the aeroplanes at 0900 hrs at about 3500 ft. We turned into the aeroplanes, which came towards us, went under us and dove for the deck. My No 4 man, Lt Aitken, called the break for my section, and I broke right and down and got onto the tail of one of the aeroplanes. After two short bursts the Me 109 caught fire and crashed in flames.'

The unit's Spitfires then fought numerous engagements over Tunisia during the next week, and on 2 December one of the 52nd FG's most distinguished future aces opened his account. Capt 'Vince' Vinson of the 2nd FS described how he downed an Fw 190 west of Bizerte;

'I gave the enemy aircraft a one-second burst. Strikes were seen as the enemy aircraft weaved through a valley, and I closed to 50 yards, striking the engine – it smoked and stopped operating. The prop began windmilling. My next burst hit the wings and the left wing then exploded, probably due to HE cannon ammunition, and the 190 went into a steep spiral. I stayed with it down to 100 ft from the ground.'

The following day Vinson combined with two RAF pilots in downing a second Fw 190, then on the 4th he waded into the escort for a formation of Ju 88s near Teboura and shot down a Bf 109G. Several other pilots made claims during this mission, including Capt Jimmie Peck, who had

The wreckage of Spitfire VC ER488 is spread over the Algerian landscape after it crashed on 17 December 1942 (*via Wojtek Matusiak*)

recently transferred to the USAAF having made 16 claims (including 3.5 destroyed) over Malta earlier in the year with Spitfire VB-equipped No 126 Sqn – he damaged one of the Ju 88s.

During the first week of December, 2nd FS pilots were credited with six destroyed, two probables and six damaged, against three losses. A few days later, however, heavy rains brought a lull in the air action for two weeks. On 19 December the 2nd FS resumed operations, and when flying near his airfield at Bone during a mid-morning patrol, Jimmie Peck spotted a trio of Fw 190s and gave chase. He eventually caught them low over the ground, at which point one of them pulled up. Despite opening fire at near maximum range, Peck's aim was true and part of his target's wing broke off. However, he was then engaged by another Fw 190 and forced to break off his attack, resulting in him only being credited with a damaged.

First USAAF Spitfire Ace

1943 opened dramatically for the 2nd FS when, on 2 January, a large force of Ju 87s, with fighter escort, attacked Bone harbour. RAF and US Spitfires scrambled in response, and 'Vince' Vinson went for a Stuka, which he hit and it exploded and broke up before crashing into the sea – his wingman, Lt John Pope, got another, and he wrote afterwards;

'Vinson and I went after two 87s that were just off the water and trailing the others. He fired a short burst at one and I fired at the other. Then we had to break because two 190s were diving on us. I saw tracers going by my head and the 190 went past just over my left wing, and close enough for me to see the colour of the pilot's eyes, if that had been of interest to me. Just after the 190s went past, we saw the 87s that we had shot at go into the water.'

Others engaged the escorts, among them Capt Jimmie Peck, who shot down an Fw 190 for his fifth victory, thus becoming the first USAAF pilot to 'make ace' whilst flying a Spitfire.

Soon afterwards, Maj Robert Levine's 4th FS replaced the squadron at Bone, with the 2nd FS moving to Biskra. To its intense frustration, the 5th FS, meanwhile, had moved to the relative backwater of Maison Blanche to provide aerial cover for the port of Algiers.

The 4th FS, meanwhile, picked up where the 2nd had left off, claiming its first success on 6 January when Maj Levine downed an Fw 190. It was his, and the squadron's, first victory. On the 14th, 1Lt Moss Fletcher, who had one shared victory from his service with the RCAF, scored his first of four kills in US colours when he downed a Bf 109 between Cap Rosa and Bone, although his fighter was damaged in the engagement and he had to bale out. Fletcher soon returned to the squadron.

On the ground, heavy fighting continued as the Anglo-American armies battled their way into Tunisia. Early the following month two squadrons from the 52nd FG moved into a waterlogged Thelepte, in Tunisia, where they relieved the badly mauled 33rd FG. The following day the group encountered the Luftwaffe, and within 48 hours Spitfires of the 31st FG had also moved into Thelepte. However, the Supermarine fighters continually suffered gun stoppages due to the blowing sand which blighted the region, thus seriously reducing the aircraft's effectiveness in combat.

The first pilot to become an ace flying the Spitfire in USAAF service was Capt Jimmie Peck of the 2nd FS, who claimed his fifth, and last, victory early on 2 January 1943 when he shot down an Fw 190 near Bone. His previous successes had come while serving with the RAF in Malta during 1942 – he is seen here in British uniform (*via Brian Cull*)

In mid February, an armoured thrust towards Kasserine by Axis forces led to an increase in demand for air support. During a lunchtime patrol on 15 February, 1Lt Jerry Collinsworth of the 307th shot down an Fw 190 to begin his journey to 'acedom'. Typical of the missions flown during this period was the operation led by 'Vince' Vinson early in the morning of the 17th, when he led a dozen Spitfires and some P-39s on an armed reconnaissance, while others hit enemy armour and guns. Allied squadrons suffered numerous losses as they vainly attempted to stop Field Marshal Erwin Rommel's *Afrika Korps* advancing beyond Kasserine and on to Thelepte, which had to be evacuated in short order, leaving a dozen unserviceable Spitfires behind.

The 31st FG fled to Tebessa and the 52nd FG to Youks-le-Bains, but both groups subsequently made several more moves. Capt Frank Hill recalled;

'We were successful in getting out of Thelepte, even though we had very little warning. I was one of the last flights to depart the base, and as we were taking off, shells were landing in the mess area in the ravine on the side of the hill.'

However, the German offensive gradually ran out of steam, and by 25 February the Allies had regained control of Kasserine, forcing Rommel back towards Tunis. US Spitfires then resumed their escort activities over the front, and it was the 31st FG's squadrons that enjoyed the most success over the next few weeks. Casualties also began to mount, and on 8 March the 307th lost two pilots in a combat south of Pichon with Fw 190s of the experienced II./JG 2. Future six-kill Spitfire ace 1Lt Jerry Collinsworth described his fight with Uffz Erich Engelbrecht, after seeing one Spitfire shot down and having initially pulled up into cloud cover to escape the pursuing Fw 190;

The commander of the 4th FS was Maj Robert Levine, who claimed all of his victories flying his personal Spitfire VC ER570/WD-Q. The latter is seen here at La Sebala in the spring of 1943 displaying a swastika for Levine's first kill, which he claimed on 8 January (*via Henry Boot*)

Spitfire VC ES306/HL-D of the 308th FS sits at Thelepte in March 1943, this airfield having been evacuated in some haste by the unit the previous month in the face of an Axis offensive. When this photograph was taken, the squadron was heavily engaged covering the US advance towards Tunis, which came under constant enemy air attack. Note how rough the ground is in the dispersal area (*F Hill via C F Shores*)

'Fortunately, when I came out of the clouds I was behind him at about 500 ft. I immediately shoved everything to the firewall and headed for him. I knew exactly when he saw me, for black smoke poured out of the FW, and I knew he had gone to full throttle. But since I had accelerated earlier than he, and had 300 ft of altitude on him, I was gaining on him. He went for the deck, which was only about 400 ft away. I wanted to avenge "Woody's" (1Lt Woodlief Thomas) death if possible, so I left Mitchell (1Lt Marlin Mitchell) and the other two FWs to their fight. The FW 190 headed in a generally southerly direction, with me gaining on him. We were flying less than 50 ft above the terrain. Shortly thereafter, as I was getting closer, the German pilot entered a steep left turn. I turned inside of him and started firing.

'One of my two 20 mm cannons jammed immediately, and the effect was to make my Spit see-saw back and forth with only one cannon firing from my wing. I don't know for sure if I hit his aircraft or not, but, in any event, he snapped inverted. I was so scared and up tight that I thought, "He's going to do a split-S and try to come up behind me". Of course he crashed into the ground doing about 350 mph. It was then that I realised that a fighter can't do a split-S from less than 50 ft above the ground at a speed of 350 mph!'

Sadly, Mitchell was shot down too.

With Axis troops in increasingly desperate straits on the ground, the enemy threw in as much air support as it could. On a late morning patrol on the 21st, the 309th FS encountered a formation of Ju 87s from III./StG 3. During the course of the action 1Lt Carl Payne achieving his second victory, as he described in his combat report;

'Our unit was flying middle position in a three-squadron escort to A-20s bombing Mezzouna airfield. The top cover (307th FS) was attacked by ME 109s just beyond the target, before the bombs were dropped. Shortly thereafter we sighted a formation of about 16 Ju 87s flying south at 4000-5000 ft. After securing permission from the bombers, I led Blue Flight down to attack from 8000 ft. I fired at one Ju 87 and saw strikes on the wings and pieces flying off. The Stuka went into a steep downward spiral, finally getting out of control at 800 ft and going straight on in. "Blue 2", Lt McCarthy, also fired on the same aircraft and saw it crash.'

It was not all sun in the desert, as evidenced by Spitfire VC VF-E of the 5th FS following a flash flood at La Sebala caused by a period of torrential rain during the spring of 1943 (*No 165 Sqn Records via P H T Green collection*)

Two other Stukas were also claimed destroyed and yet more damaged. Elsewhere that same day, the 52nd FG was in action, losing aircraft to JG 51's Bf 109Gs. However, 24 hours later a number of the 4th FS's future aces made claims in a fight with yet more Messerschmitt fighters over Mezzouna. 1Lt Robert E Armstong shot one down (the first of his four victories), while the man ultimately destined to be the leading USAAF Spitfire pilot made his first claim when another Bf 109G fell to the guns of 1Lt Sylvan Feld. Also successful was 1Lt Victor Cabas, who shot a German fighter down for his third successful combat, while 1Lt Moss Fletcher also claimed the third of his victories.

In the same area in mid-afternoon, the 2nd FS, now commanded by Capt 'Vince' Vinson, was in action, and Capt Norman McDonald achieved the first of his 11.5 victories when he despatched a pair of Ju 88s;

'I saw the enemy aircraft at about 1000 ft above us, and I climbed directly up at them. They were flying a two-ship formation slightly echeloned to the right. I levelled off behind and slightly below their No 2 ship. From 50 yards, with five degrees deflection to the right, I opened up with cannon and machine guns. My first cannon shells knocked his right motor out and the engine caught fire. Then the cannon shells exploded in the cockpit and along the fuselage, and the whole ship seemed to explode in mid air. It went down burning. In all, I gave him about four seconds of cannons and machine guns.

'I then closed on the No 1 aircraft, who apparently had not seen me yet, and from a range of 25 yards I opened up with a four-second burst of cannons and machine guns. I set his right motor on fire, his right wing dropped and my cannon fire hit his left motor, setting it on fire also. Then I saw several other strikes of cannon fire along his fuselage. The aeroplane went into a spin towards the ground. I then looked round and saw the first Ju 88 hit the ground in flames.'

During a very successful day, the 52nd FG had claimed nine destroyed, and McDonald had established himself on the path to 'acedom'. Support to US ground forces remained the priority, however, and 23 March was a particularly busy day. During a combat shortly before 1000 hrs, Capt Sweetland's Spitfire collided with a Bf 109G and both crashed. The latter aircraft was flown by *experte* Maj Joachim Müncheberg of *Stab./*JG 77, who, moments earlier, had shot down a Spitfire for his 135th, and last, victory.

Ground support missions continued the next day, and whilst patrolling over the Maknassy basin that afternoon, Spitfires of the 2nd FS found a formation of Ju 88s, escorted by Fw 190s. The Spitfires dived on the German aircraft and squadron CO, Capt 'Vince' Vinson, selected a Focke-Wulf fighter and opened fire from close range. He later noted that 'the enemy aircraft lost speed very quickly and caught fire, emitting a volume of black smoke out of the exhausts. I pulled away after almost colliding with it'. In spite of his close call, it was Vinson's fifth success, so making him the USAAF's third Spitfire ace, but the first to make all his claims with an American unit.

The 31st FG also remained busy, and during the late afternoon of 25 March Lt Col Fred Dean led a sweep of the La Fauconnerie area. At 7000 ft over the Faid Pass, a solitary Fw 190 was sighted below and down sun of the Spitfires, so Capt Frank Hill of the 308th was ordered to engage it. Approaching unseen from out of the sun, he shot it down in

Capt Arnold Vinson of the 2nd FS made his first claims on 2 December 1942, when he damaged a Bf 109 and then shot down an Fw 190 west of Bizerte. 'I gave the enemy aircraft a one-second burst. Strikes were seen as the enemy aircraft weaved through a valley and I closed to 50 yards, striking the engine, and it smoked and stopped operating'. Vinson became an ace on the evening of 24 March 1943, but on 3 April, having destroyed a Ju 87, he was jumped by a Bf 109 and killed (*via Norman Franks*)

Spitfire VC ER256 was the personal aircraft of 31st FG CO Lt Col Fred M Dean, who adopted the RAF practice of carrying his initials on his fighter (*via Brian Cull*)

flames in front of the whole group for his second victory. The 309th was successful four days later when, near Gafsa, it was attacked by nine enemy fighters, and in the subsequent fight an Fw 190 and a Bf 109 were shot down, the former by Maj Harrison Thyng for his third confirmed kill.

— ADVANCE TO TUNIS —

By 1 April the enemy had been roundly beaten at Mareth by the British 8th Army and forced to retreat north, while the US Army's II Corps continued to push eastwards towards the Maknassy basin.

Lt Col Dean led the 31st FG throughout the North African campaign, and claimed his only victory during the Pantelleria operation (*via Brian Cull*)

The latter's advance was continually hampered by effective Axis air attacks, however, with the Luftwaffe's Ju 87 units proving particularly troublesome. As a result, both Spitfire groups flew standing patrols over the advancing US troops, and they were soon in action against Bf 109Gs from II./JG 77 that were attempting to protect the vulnerable Stukas. A number of USAAF pilots claimed victories on 1 April, including the 309th's CO, Harrison Thyng, who downed a Bf 109G, while squadronmate 1Lt Carl Payne was credited with a Messerschmitt fighter probably destroyed.

Spitfires of the 52nd FG were also engaged during the day when, shortly after noon, SSgt James E Butler (one of the relatively few NCO fighter pilots in the USAAF), who was helping to cover troops near Hamadt, spotted an Fw 190 above him. The latter promptly dived to ground level as Butler gave chase through the hills, and the American pilot scored hits and saw it pour with smoke. He did not see it crash, however, and Butler was only credited with a probable.

Later that same day the 52nd FG intercepted a formation of Ju 88s over El Guettar and five were shot down, including one by 1Lt Sylvan Feld of the 4th FS, while Capt Norman McDonald of the 2nd FS shared another with Capt George Williams. Also in action was SSgt Butler, who attacked the same aircraft as Lt Sanborn. The latter wrote afterwards in his report, 'I saw Butler go into clouds after him. Then the enemy aircraft came out of clouds in a dive, with its right engine and the right side of the fuselage in flames. The enemy aircraft went into a spin and crashed into a

The 2nd FS's Capt Norman McDonald, from North Carolina, reached 'acedom' in spectacular fashion on the evening of 3 April 1943 when he downed three of the thirteen Ju 87 Stukas from III./StG 3 claimed destroyed over El Gutar by American Spitfires. He was one of the leading USAAF Spitfire pilots, with 7.5 of his eventual total of 11.5 kills being claimed with the British fighter (*via Norman Franks*)

mountain and exploded just south of Djebel Hamadt'. This share was the first of Butler's five victory claims. These Ju 88 kills had come at some cost, as several Spitfires were also shot down.

Two days later the 52nd FG had an even greater success which was a source of some satisfaction, as there had been criticism from the Army about the level of air support it had been recently receiving. Late in the afternoon, the 2nd FS, led by Capt Vinson, set off to patrol the frontline. It soon came across a formation of around 14 Ju 87s, with a Bf 109 escort, and as the Americans dived to attack, the Stukas jettisoned their bombs and desperately scattered before their escort could intervene. The US squadron subsequently claimed 13 Ju 87s destroyed, and although there was undoubtedly an element of double claiming, they had achieved a significant success – but a tragic price had been paid.

Capt Norman McDonald, who shot down three of the dive-bombers, graphically described the action in his combat report;

'As my flight was nearest the Stukas, we went after the farthest formation. They were very slow, so we caught them easily. I closed to within 25-30 yards of the trailing Ju 87 and opened up with both cannons and machine guns, using about five degrees of deflection. A two- to three-second burst was sufficient. The motor belched black smoke and slight flame. The aircraft dove down to the left and flew straight into the ground from about 1000 ft. I closed to the same distance on the next Stuka, and using a similar angle of deflection, opened up with both cannons and machine guns in three-second bursts. The aircraft erupted in flames and broke into pieces in the air. This combat took place at 1000 ft.

'The third victim was about 500 yards ahead. I closed on him easily. He was in a slight climb. Again, my range was no more than 35 yards, with very slight right deflection from slightly below. The rear gunner was firing intensely at me. I opened up with cannon and machine guns, again firing three-second bursts. Just as we entered a cloud, great chunks of his propeller and parts of the aeroplane flew back, just missing me. When I came out of the cloud, the Stuka was spinning into the ground, emitting much smoke and with pieces still flying off.'

Also flying with McDonald's Blue Flight was SSgt James Butler, who claimed two of the Stukas destroyed.

Their CO, Capt Arnold Vinson, also downed a Ju 87 to take his tally to 5.333 victories, but as he chased a Bf 109 that was approaching McDonald, he was himself shot down and killed. This was a terrible blow for the 2nd FS, as Vinson had been a charismatic, and successful, leader. His No 2, Lt Miles Lynn, described his demise. 'I was with Vinson when we were jumped by 109s. He had already shot down one Stuka. I called "Break!", but he was hit as we turned'. Back at base, Norman McDonald said, 'To those who flew with him as their leader, he was the best'. Vinson was replaced by Maj George Williams.

The enemy was not giving in easily, however, and on 4 April Spitfires from the 52nd FG were in action over La Fauconnerie with yet more Bf 109Gs from III./JG 77, and the American pilots emerged with three kills to their credit. In return, one of the Luftwaffe's great *experte* (with more than 150 kills to his credit), Maj Johannes 'Makki' Steinhoff, who was also the *Geschwaderkommodore* of JG 77, shot down the Spitfire of newly-arrived Lt Richard East.

During the 9 April action against Ju 88s, the 2nd FS's 1Lt John Aitken claimed a half-share to add to the Bf 109 he had shot down near La Fauconnerie two days earlier. These were his only claims with the Spitfire, but he took his total to 4.5 destroyed in September 1944 when flying P-51s with the 503rd FS (*52nd FW*)

During a big fight over Kairouan on 9 April 1943, the 52nd FG claimed 11 victories and 1Lt Vic Cabas became an ace. Future aces 1Lts Feld, Ohr and Aitken and SSgt Butler also claimed. One casualty, however, was 1Lt Eugene Steinbrenner, whose Spitfire VC ER120/VF-D of the 5th FS crash-landed on a ridge following flak damage, but it was later recovered (*via Harry Holmes*)

Allied fighter units then began a concerted effort (codenamed Operation *Flax*) against the enemy's air re-supply train flying into Tunisia, during which 1Lt John A Carey claimed the first of his 4.5 victories when he destroyed a Bf 109 near El Guettar. The group moved northeast to Sbeitla shortly afterwards.

On 6 April the 8th Army broke through the Wadi Akarit line, and the following day its advanced units linked with II Corps, which by now had reached Mezzouna. Later that month, in the north, the British 1st Army began its spring offensive. During heavy air fighting over Tunisia, the 52nd FG lost six Spitfires to fighters or flak.

Returning to 6 April, early that day 11 aircraft from the 307th escorted A-20s sent to bomb La Fouconnerie, and en route to the target they were attacked by a dozen Bf 109Gs shortly after 0730 hrs. Lt Virgil Fields fired off all his ammunition at one of the fighters, and had the satisfaction of seeing part of the port wing of his victim fall off. He was duly credited with the first of his six victories upon returning to base, his victim believed to have been Ltn Klaas.

The following day, again near La Fauconnerie, two Bf 109Gs were shot down, including one by the 2nd FS's 1Lt John Aitken for his first victory – he became an ace later in the war, having by then been promoted to the rank of major. Another pilot continued his path to 'acedom' 24 hours later when 1Lt Sylvan Feld of the 4th FS destroyed a Bf 109G northwest of Kairouan.

Feld's fourth victory came on 9 April as the Allied advance continued from the south and the west in the face of stiff opposition both on the ground and in the air. Early that evening, squadrons from the 52nd FG had intercepted two formations of Ju 88s without escort near Kairouan, some 30 miles inland to the west of Sousse. For the loss of two Spitfires, the group claimed 11 destroyed, including one each to 1Lts Sylvan Feld and Fred Ohr (from the 2nd FS). Ohr later became the only US ace of Korean ancestry, and his first victory was also his only success with the Spitfire – his remaining five kills came in 1944 in P-51B/Ds.

The honours on the 9th, however, went to the 4th FS's 1Lt Vic Cabas, who took his total to five victories, thus making him the latest American to achieve ace status flying the British thoroughbred fighter. Also elevated to 'acedom' was SSgt Butler, who shot down a Ju 88 and shared in the destruction of a second with 1Lt John Aitken. With three and two shared victories, Jim Butler thus became the only USAAF NCO pilot to 'make ace' flying Spitfires. The fight was not one-sided, however, as Capt McDonald was hit, although fortunately not seriously.

On the 12th Sousse fell, and the Allied armies converged on the Kairouan area. Within two days the 8th Army had reached the foot of the Atlas Mountains at Enfidaville, and as the Allies began the final advance on Tunis, air action subsided a little.

An American ex-Spitfire pilot also became an ace soon afterwards on Sunday, 18 April in the climax of Operation *Flax*. Although no USAAF Spitfires were involved in the action, one of the successful pilots that day was 2Lt MacArthur Powers, flying a P-40 Warhawk of the 314th FS. He had previously flown Spitfire VBs over the desert with the RAF's No 145 Sqn in 1942, and had claimed two and one shared victories with the unit prior to transferring to the USAAF in January 1943. During the evening of what became famous as the 'Palm Sunday Massacre' over the Gulf of Tunis, he shot down four Ju 52/3m transports, as well as one of their escorting Bf 109Gs, to reach 'acedom' in some style!

Another ex-RAF Spitfire pilot to attain ace status in a similar manner in the P-40 during that same mission was 2Lt Arthur Cleaveland of the 66th FS, who shot down no fewer than five Ju 52/3ms.

About an hour earlier, Spitfires of the 4th FS had been engaged some 20 miles east of Tunis, and 1Lt Sylvan Feld shot down an Fw 190 to also be elevated to ace status – he had claimed all five of his victories with the British fighter. Feld was successful again the next day when the 4th FS conducted a bomber escort mission to Tunis. About 20 miles north of the city the unit was attacked by enemy fighters, one of which forced down 1Lt Edwin Smith near Mateur. However, Sylvan Feld claimed an Fw 190, and also shot a Bf 109G off Smith's tail, as the ace later recalled in his combat report;

'After the bombers left the target area, our six Spitfires spotted four Focke-Wulfs down low. We dived at them, and in the attack that

31st FG XO, Lt Col Ames, formates over a choppy Mediterranean Sea off the Tunisian coast in Spitfire VC JK226/HL-AA of the 308th FS during the spring of 1943 (*via Wojtek Matusiak*)

followed I closed on one, and after firing saw the pilot bale out as the bullets struck the cockpit. During this fracas another of our pilots was suddenly attacked by six Me 109s. One got directly on his tail. I turned inside him and fired. He exploded on the first burst. We were right above the ground at the time, and they were throwing flak up at us by the bushel.'

Feld's CO, Maj Robert Levine, who was flying his regular aircraft (the spectacularly marked Spitfire VB ER570/WD-Q), shot down

Another successful pilot with the 4th FS was Capt Moss Fletcher, who claimed his first (shared) victory when flying with the RCAF. During his time with the 4th FS he was credited with a further four kills to become an ace in late April 1943. Fletcher's aircraft not only carried his name and score, but also his personal nose art. Fletcher's crew chief is seen here sitting on the wing of their Spitfire (*52nd FW*)

During the spring of 1943, quantities of the improved Spitfire IX began being delivered to the USAAF in North Africa. Among those sent to the 4th FS was EN354/WD-W, which was christened *Doris June II* by its pilot, 1Lt Leonard V Helton. He claimed two victories in April and August 1943 (*ww2images*)

another for his second victory, while a third Bf 109G was shared by 1Lts Vic Cabas, who made his final claim, and John Blythe.

By now the Allies had formed a complete ring around the Axis forces, which were trapped against the sea – the end in Africa was in sight, although much hard fighting in the mountains was still to be done.

The writing was on the wall though, and soon after breakfast on 20 April, II./JG 51 began evacuating Tunisia for Sicily. However, some of its fighters became involved with Spitfires of the 4th FS, forcing the Messerschmitt pilots to jettison their long range tanks and dive away for their lives. Robert Levine was again successful when he downed a Bf 109G over Tunis, although this third victory would also prove to be his last. Several other pilots also made claims, including Moss Fletcher, who destroyed two to take his total to 4.5 kills, and thus make him the 4th FS's third ace. Sadly, however, amongst those lost was SSgt Jim Butler, who was killed.

At about this time some Spitfire VIIIs and IXs began to be issued to both USAAF groups, and 2nd FS ace Capt Norman McDonald enthused about them. 'The Spit IX was a different breed of cat. With a four-bladed steel propeller, bigger engine and manoeuvring characteristics similar to the Spit V, the newer Spit IX was much faster'.

It was whilst flying one of the new Spitfire IXs, on 21 April, that future five-kill ace 1Lt John White of the 307th FS, who had first seen action over Dieppe, became embroiled with more than a dozen German fighters. In a confused dogfight, he succeeded in shooting down a Bf 109G for his first victory. During another sweep later in the day, White, again in a Spitfire IX, shot down an Fw 190.

On 22 April, the 309th FS's Capt Frank Hill, also flying a Spitfire IX, was escorting USAAF P-40s when, at 18,000 ft over Pont du Fahs, they spotted six Bf 109Gs attacking Spitfires from the 52nd FG. Hill chased down one of the enemy fighters, and after firing on it, the Messerschmitt emitted a heavy trail of black smoke and dived away. The German aircraft subsequently crashed after 1Lt Rahn had also fired at it. Hill was then approached by another Bf 109G, as he recalled years later;

'I mistook an Me 109 for one of my Spits, and this mistake almost cost me my life, but I was fortunate that the old Spit could "turn on a dime". Even though the canopy popped from the rails when I yanked back on the stick, I was able, after a turn or so, to roll out onto him as he hit the deck.'

The Messerschmitt eventually streamed thick black smoke and was claimed as a probable.

On a sweep later that afternoon, Hill was again in the thick of the action, as was future ace 1Lt Carl Payne, who recalled;

'I was leading my squadron on a P-40 escort mission. We were attacked by three Me 109s from above. We broke into them, and I fired a one-second burst from 30 degrees astern at 150 yards at one enemy aircraft. Immediately, dense white smoke poured out of the Me 109. It seemed to go out of control, going right on into the ground, streaming white smoke continuously. Lt McAbee saw the aircraft crash.'

Frank Hill also attacked it, and so the victory was shared.

By 1 May the Allied armies were poised for the final assault in North Africa, with the 8th Army in the south and the 1st Army set to advance along the north coast of Tunisia to capture Bizerte. US and French troops gained the first big breakthrough the next day when they took Mateur.

6 May was to be a very busy day for Allied fighters, as before dawn the 1st Army launched a direct attack on Tunis. The Spitfires of the 31st FG saw some intensive action during ten sweeps that day, the various engagements fought by the units producing the group's first aces. During one such mission in the middle of the day, recently promoted Maj Frank Hill, who was leading the 309th FS in a new Spitfire IX, clashed with Bf 109Gs;

'On the morning mission, I was leading the Spit IXs. That was the newer Spitfire with the bigger engine, and I chased two ME-109s around the sky, finally getting one which dove head-on into the ground north of Tunis. Just a little before this, I followed one ME-109 north towards Bizerte and shot at him, and he continued to dive, with black smoke coming out all the way down. There was another ME-109 on our tail, so we had to turn to head into it to avoid getting hit. Just as I turned back, I saw a large explosion where the first ME-109 had been headed, so I believe he went in also. His demise was later confirmed by my wingman.'

Hill's first victim thus made the 24-year-old New Yorker the group's premier ace. Two hours later, future ace 1Lt Jerry Collinsworth of the 307th FS also encountered German fighters;

'I pulled up behind the No 2 man, fired a short burst, and when I did the canopy came off the FW-190. I quit firing, as I assumed he was getting ready to bale out, and sure enough, out he came. I decided to go back and take a look at him. As I passed him, for some reason I thumbed my nose at the old boy. It seems kinda silly now, I know, but I still think it was a lot better than shooting him in his parachute. I'm sure he thought so too.'

This was Collinsworth's fourth victory, while another future ace of the 307th, 1Lt Charles Fischette, also shot down a Bf 109G for his second victory.

At around 1600 hrs, the 31st FG mounted yet another sweep over Tunis, and one of the pilots involved was Maj Frank Hill. He later recalled in his combat report;

'We ran into about 16 ME-109s and Macchi 202s. There were six of us in Spit Vs and four above us in Spit IXs. I started after this formation, came up from underneath where they didn't see us and shot at one Macchi, which I hit. He immediately half-rolled and started down. I don't know if he crashed or pulled out. I just damaged it. Their formation then split up, and so did ours, and we fought a general dogfight.

A smiling 1Lt Jerry Collinsworth poses for the camera in the North African sun. He claimed four victories during the fighting over Tunisia in the spring of 1943, and subsequently became an ace during the bombardment of Pantelleria in early June (*31st FW*)

'Maj Kelly, who was a new replacement, was my wingman. He stayed with me, even though he lagged behind a couple of times, because he was in a much slower aeroplane. When we sighted some more ME-109s and gave chase, two of them turned off and climbed into the sun. We went after them, underneath and behind, so they didn't see us. When we were able to close in again, I opened fire on the lead one when they both half-rolled, and he went straight down trailing glycol and smoke. Maj Kelly watched him for a long while, and believed he never did come out of the dive.

'The other ME-109 straightened out right away, and I came up on his tail and fired what little ammunition I had left at him. Kelly shot at him too, and then we both broke away. The German must have known I was out of ammunition, because he turned right back and started after us. He was almost on Kelly's tail when I told my No 2 to break hard left. The ME-109 overshot us and never did attack us again. We were down to our last few gallons of gas, so we landed at an emergency field near the front, re-serviced and came on home.'

Although Maj Hill had identified both Macchi and Messerschmitt fighters, his flight had probably engaged 14 Macchi C.202s of 7° *Gruppo*, which had in turn made a number of claims. The Italians lost Capitano Sergio Maurer, and the *Gruppo* commander, Tenente Colonnello Giovanni Zapetta, crash-landed. Maj Hill was duly credited with a Bf 109 destroyed and a C.202 and a second Messerschmitt fighter damaged.

Future 309th FS seven-kill ace 1Lt Dale Shafer also shot down a C.202 from 7° *Gruppo* for his second victory, whilst his old CO, the recently-promoted Lt Col Harrison Thyng, claimed a Bf 109 to become the 31st FG's third ace that day. This proved to be the latter pilot's final Spitfire claim.

Yet another ace to see action on 6 May was 1Lt Carl Payne, again from the 309th FS, who subsequently wrote;

'I was leading Blue Flight of my squadron on a fighter sweep of the battle area when we were engaged by two Me 109s. The enemy aircraft passed us head on and then half-rolled. I followed the leader down and closed to 300 yards, opening fire with both machine guns and cannons. I closed to point blank range, firing a series of two-second bursts. I saw strikes on the wings and fuselage, and white smoke streamed out. As I overshot the enemy aircraft, it made several sharp turns. I followed, and fired short bursts when possible. After the second turn, the Me 109 flew into the ground. The combat took place almost at ground level.'

Spitfire VC ER187/WZ-C of the 309th FS was flown by unit CO Maj Frank Hill on the afternoon of 6 May 1943, when, during a sweep of the Tunis area, he destroyed a Bf 109 and damaged a second Messerschmitt fighter and an Italian C.202 (*F Hill via C F Shores*)

Maj Frank Hill poses alongside Spitfire ER187, which bears his victory total and both he and his wife's names (*F Hill via C F Shores*)

4th FS Spitfire VC ES138/WD-N sits on a dusty Tunisian airfield during the summer of 1943, prior to the group moving north to Sicily (*ww2 images*)

The 31st FG's tally of 11 aircraft shot down on 6 May 1943 set a record in the North African theatre for the most fighters destroyed by an American fighter group in a single day to date.

During the afternoon of 8 May, the 'Desert Rats' of the British 7th Armoured Division entered Tunis, and soon afterwards the US 9th Infantry Division captured Bizerte. A rapid armoured thrust sealed the bulk of the remaining Axis forces in the Cap Bon peninsula, and the last remaining German and Italian fighters evacuated Tunisia the next day. A number of other Axis aircraft were shot down attempting to flee on the 9th, with Spitfire pilots from the 5th FS enjoying a particularly successful early morning action which resulted in six Bf 109Gs being claimed destroyed, including two by 1Lt Walter Morgan.

Several hours later, near Beni Khalled, 1Lt John Carey also shot a fighter down, and shared in the destruction of another to continue his path to 'acedom'. His Spitfire was hit by flak just minutes later, however, forcing him to crash-land. Fortunately, Carey met an Arab who helped him evade German patrols, and he was picked up by British troops and returned to his unit.

These proved to be the final USAAF Spitfire victories of the North African campaign before all resistance ceased and Italian Gen Giovanni Messe surrendered the last Axis forces in Africa on the 13 May.

During this hard fought campaign, the two USAAF Spitfire groups had claimed 133 victories against 90 losses, some of which were due to flak or weather. With seven confirmed victories in North Africa, 1Lt Sylvan Feld of the 4th FS had emerged as the most successful USAAF Spitfire pilot in-theatre.

Shortly after the fall of Tunisia the 52nd FG was transferred to the control of the North African Coastal Air Force for shipping protection and defensive duties.

WITH THE DESERT AIR FORCE

A number of American pilots flying Spitfires with the RAF in North Africa had preceded the arrival of the 31st and 52nd FGs by some months. The first Spitfires had joined the Desert Air Force in mid-1942 with the arrival of No 145 Sqn in Egypt. One of its pilots was Sgt MacArthur Powers from Long Island, who had previously flown Spitfires with No 91 Sqn in England. He recorded his thoughts on arrival. 'North

Africa, the desert, sand and sweat, the blue, ever so blue, sky and the vast distances we could see over the "Med" were a great contrast to England. This was my bowl of fish, and I loved every minute of it!'

Powers made his first claim on 27 August in the fighting on the Alamein line when he attacked a Ju 88 about 15 miles to the south of El Alamein, although he almost missed his target. 'I was delayed in making my attack just long enough for me to see the rear end of a Ju 88 – the only one I had seen. Much to my amazement, it did not fall apart when I hit it with cannon. In fact it may still be flying around for all I know. This taught me to get in close, and I always did after that'. Then, two months later, on 23 October, Powers achieved his first victory during a sweep to El Daba at the start of the Battle of El Alamein when he shot down a Bf 109.

Powers also recalled details of his usual aircraft. 'My mother's name was Jessica. This was shortened to Jessy, and I had this painted on the right side of the engine nacelle. *Jessy 4* was my last Spitfire'. He had several further successes, including one Bf 109 destroyed and a second shared destroyed, in the first week of November 1942, prior to transferring to the USAAF's 324th FG on 3 January 1943 and claiming more victories flying the P-40 in the MTO.

The pilot with possibly the most spectacular run of success over the desert at this time was Flt Lt John 'Crash' Curry of No 601 Sqn, which had moved from Malta to Egypt in June 1942. During two separate sorties over Burg el Arab on 1 September, he destroyed two Bf 109Fs. Then a week later he shot down another Messerschmitt, which is believed to have been the aircraft flown by Knight's Cross holder, and 55-victory ace, Oblt Hans-Arnold Stahlschmidt, who was killed. The shared destruction of a Ju 88 on 29 September took him to 'acedom', and in the intense fighting during the Battle of El Alamein the following month, Curry made six more claims, including three destroyed, to take his final total to 7.333 victories. Rested between November 1942 and June 1943, he then completed a further tour on Spitfires as CO No 80 Sqn.

The most successful American pilot to serve with the RAF was Lance Wade, who, whilst flying Hurricanes over the desert with No 33 Sqn in 1941-42, was credited with 12 and 2 shared victories. In mid-January 1943 he joined No 145 Sqn, and had become its CO just as the unit began a period of heavy fighting.

On 25 February, German artillery fire ranged in on No 145 Sqn's Castel Benito airfield, and a hasty scramble began to save the aircraft. Wade's Spitfire VB had its starboard wing damaged by an exploding shell, but he nevertheless managed to fly it to El Assa and safely land the fighter.

The heavily moustached Wade, nicknamed 'Wildcat', soon began adding to his tally of kills, claiming a Bf 109G on 1 March for his first Spitfire victory. He made six more claims, including three destroyed,

One of the Americans who flew Spitfires in the desert with the RAF was Flt Sgt MacArthur Powers of No 145 Sqn, who used Spitfire VC BR390/ZX-N on 2 November 1942 to damage a Bf 109 (*P H T Green collection*)

The pilots of No 145 Sqn's attached Polish Fighting Team use Spitfire VC ES252/ZX-E as the backdrop for a group photograph. The aircraft was flown by unit CO, Sqn Ldr Lance Wade, during March 1943, and he used it to down a Bf 109 on the 22nd of that month, having also made two earlier claims with the fighter (*via Wojtek Matusiak*)

before the end of the month. As the enemy front collapsed in April, Wade, who was by now flying a Spitfire IX, kept himself busy adding a further four Axis fighters to his tally. The first of these was the Bf 109G which he brought down near Medenine on the 4th, killing pilot Fw Ertl of 3./JG 53. Wade claimed another Messerschmitt on 22 April, a C.202 five days later and, finally, yet another Bf 109G on the 30th – his final kill of the North African fighting.

Wade's victory on the last day of April 1943 was not, however, the final aerial success to be claimed by an American in an RAF Spitfire over North Africa. On 1 May, No 33 Sqn's Flt Lt Oliver 'Sandy' Kallio from Ironwood, Michigan, shot down a Ju 88 of III./KG 26 for his third victory whilst flying on an escort mission from Bersis over convoy *Liquid*. Although Kallio did not ultimately become an ace, his final tally numbered nine claims, including four destroyed.

It was whilst flying a No 33 Sqn Spitfire VC from Bersis (like ER335/RS-O and ER337/RS-J) that Flt Lt 'Sandy' Kallio claimed the last victory by an American in an RAF Spitfire in the North African campaign when, on 1 May 1943, he shot down a Ju 88 from III./KG 26 whilst escorting convoy *Liquid* in the Mediterranean (*M Naydler*)

OVER MEDITERRANEAN ISLANDS

T he first Americans to fly Spitfires in the Mediterranean were amongst a number of RAF pilots that had arrived on Malta on 21 March 1942, having ferried fighters in from the aircraft carrier HMS *Eagle*, as recalled by Sqn Ldr Laddie Lucas of No 249 Sqn. 'The American pilots, I remember, were a damn good lot – there's no doubt that they really were an absolutely super bunch. With those guys, it was the "art of the possible". They were so positive that I admired them tremendously'.

Attack after attack was launched on Malta by Axis aircraft, with the offensive proving unrelenting in the spring and summer of 1942. The new-comers were thrown straight into the action, and included in their number were two ex-No 121 Sqn pilots, Plt Offs Jim Peck and Don McLeod. On 22 March, Peck, who was described as 'dark and small, and a first class fighter pilot', made his initial claim over the island when he damaged a Ju 88. Two days later both he and McLeod brought down a Bf 109 apiece, with the latter pilot repeating the feat the following day. However, on 2 April McLeod was forced to bale out, as he vividly described;

'Four of us went up to meet 24 Me 109s escorting bombers on a daylight attack. I thought I was all right until I saw stuff flying around me like a horizontal hailstorm. Then I knew I was for it. My Spitfire was shot up so badly that the right aileron was sticking up vertically and the elevators were disabled.'

After further attacks, McLeod baled out wounded.

Another former 'Eagle' who arrived in late April, having ferried Spitfires off USS *Wasp*, was Plt Off Reade Tilley from Florida. At 6 ft 4 in tall, he made an immediate impression, being well thought of. Indeed, Laddie Lucas described him as 'a warm, gregarious, soft spoken southerner. A highly skilled and dedicated man, you couldn't help but like him'. Tilley and Peck rapidly made names for themselves, becoming the first Americans to win the DFC over the battered island. And like Peck and McLeod before him, Tilley too was quickly in the action, damaging a Bf 109 on 28 April. After four months of hectic fighting Tilley left Malta with seven destroyed, three probables and six damaged to his credit.

In early May 1942, the so-called 'American Flight' was formed within No 126 Sqn, with Plt Off Jimmie Peck as the flight commander. The other pilots were Don McLeod, Reade Tilley, Doug Booth, Fred Almos, Sunday McHan and Brice Downs.

On 20 May Peck was awarded a DFC, having made 15 claims since arriving in Malta – 3$^1/_2$ destroyed, three probables and no less than eight

Plt Off Donald McLeod of No 126 Sqn arrived in Malta on 21 March 1942 and shot down two Bf 109s on the 24th and 25th of the month. However, he was himself shot down in flames on 2 April and baled out, injured. McLeod later transferred to the USAAF, and scored two more victories with the 83rd FS (*via Brian Cull*)

damaged. He survived more than forty combats over Malta, and later spoke to American reporters of his experiences;

'I never even got a scratch or so much as a bullet through my aeroplane. In all the fighting I haven't received so much as a scratch. Anyhow, I have been lucky, I never fly without this lucky wristwatch.'

The 'American Flight' was soon joined by another future ace, Plt Off 'Rip' Jones, who, on the morning of the 18th, opened his account by shooting down a Bf 109 that was strafing a rescue launch. He shared another that evening. Reade Tilley too had been scoring steadily, and on the morning of 23 May he shot down a Macchi to claim his fifth victory, thus becoming the first American Spitfire ace over the beleaguered island.

Other Spitfire units on Malta also had a sprinkling of Americans, with Texan Sgt Merriwell Vineyard of the RCAF serving with No 185 Sqn and future ace Flt Sgt Arthur Cleaveland, from Springfield, Ohio, being a part of No 601 Sqn. The latter damaged a Bf 109 over Malta on 10 May for his only claim with the RAF. Also joining No 601 Sqn from the next *Wasp* ferry run, in June, was 26-year-old Texan Flg Off John 'Crash' Curry, whose subsequent exploits in North Africa were detailed in the previous chapter. Whilst in Malta, Curry quickly made his mark, being described by his flight commander, 5.5-kill ace Flt Lt Denis Barnham, 'as slightly built, suntanned and moustached. He was having the time of his life, although he complained incessantly that it was time the squadron got some pilots who wouldn't desert him every time he led them into a dogfight'.

No 185 Sqn's 'Tex' Vineyard, who later became a six-kill ace flying Hellcats over the Pacific with VF-2 from USS *Hornet* in 1944, had a torrid time during one engagement on 16 June, as No 185 Sqn's diary recorded;

'The boys went up looking for ME 109s. They found what they were looking for – 12 ME 109s coming down from the sun. Four Spitfires broke in all directions. Flt Sgt Vineyard pulled out of a spiral dive and his seat promptly came loose and pinned him against the dashboard. "Tex" had to bale out, and had some trouble getting loose from his machine. However, he managed to trade his flying boot for his life, and he came floating down mouthing uncouth Texan oaths. "Tex" was none the worse for the enforced swim.'

The first of the Americans to receive the DFC whilst on Malta was Plt Off Reade Tilley of No 126 Sqn, who received his award from the island's Governor, Lord Gort (*JSCSC*)

With the arrival of a significant number of former 'Eagle' squadron pilots in Malta, an 'American Flight' was formed within No 126 Sqn at Luqa in May 1942. Among the squadron's aircraft was Spitfire VC BR471/MK-P, which was shot down by Bf 109s in mid-October 1942 (*C R Long*)

45

Second in the rankings as the most successful American Spitfire pilot was 19-year-old Plt Off Claude Weaver III of No 185 Sqn, who, in a little over six weeks, was credited with 10.5 victories (*via Brian Cull*)

Vineyard made his only claim with the RAF a week later when he damaged a Bf 109.

Shortly after Vineyard's brush with death, one of the greatest American exponents of the Spitfire joined No 185 Sqn when Sgt Claude Weaver from Oklahoma City arrived just as the intensity of the air fighting reached its peak, and the privations on Malta increased.

On 15 July, 31 Spitfires were flown off HMS *Eagle*, with two of them being piloted by Americans Sgts V H Wynn and J L Lowry (both NCOs in the RCAF). The men were assigned to the experienced No 249 Sqn, where Wynn soon began making a name for himself, although five days after arriving he was hit by fire from a Bf 109 and slightly wounded.

On the 17th Claude Weaver began his path to ace status, as the unit's unofficial diary recorded. '"Shorty" Reid with Sgt Weaver, one of the new boys, each accounted for a 109F type. The boys also escorted the high-speed launch that went out of its way to pick up the Jerries'. Weaver was successful again five days later, as the diarist continued. 'Sgt Weaver maintained his good work, this time shooting down two nasty ME 109Fs'. The following day Weaver saw yet more action. 'A Flight went to town on a plot of 15+, Sgt Weaver scoring another double – 2 ME 109s again – a really excellent record'. All this success had come in less than a week, the youthful American 'making ace' three weeks short of his 19th birthday!

During the late afternoon of 26 July, Flg Off 'Rip' Jones from No 126 Sqn intercepted a Ju 88 some 30 miles to the north of Malta and shot it down, thus securing ace status. Malta's skies were deadly, however, and at the end of July fellow ace Weaver was attacked by one of the Luftwaffe's leading *experte* in the Mediterranean, Oblt Gerhard Michalski of II./JG 53. The American duly became his 41st victim when Weaver was forced to crash-land his shot up Spitfire.

Malta's situation was by now critical, and in early August the massive Operation *Pedestal* convoy sailed from Gibraltar at the start of an epic battle with, amongst other materiel, more Spitfires to be flown off. Amongst the pilots was another former 'Eagle', Plt Off 'Art' Roscoe, who was to end up with eight claims, including two destroyed. On the morning of the 13th, the battered convoy came within range of Malta's Spitfires which were in action throughout the day.

One patrol mid afternoon encountered reconnaissance Ju 88 F6+KK of 2(F)./122, flown by Uffz H-J Schmiedgen, at 14,000 ft 15 miles west of Linosa. 'Georgia' Wynn followed Plt Off 'Rip' Jones in and scored hits on the fuselage, before Canadian ace Plt Off George Beurling delivered the coup de grace. This share in the destruction of the Ju 88 gave Wynn his first confirmed success, as Beurling described in his diary. 'I saw "Georgia" go in head-on and pull up over the bomber, which just kept plowing along, straight ahead – the best thing it could do in the circumstances'.

Although still being regularly bombed, the crisis had largely passed for Malta, allowing an increasing number of offensive sorties to be mounted. On 9 September Claude Weaver, who had recently received the DFM, joined his squadron on a sweep over Comiso airfield, in Sicily. Having shot down a Macchi fighter, his engine failed and he force-landed with one wing on a beach and the other in the water to become a PoW. Then, on 17 October, in an action fought early in the morning during the final

Flg Off 'Woody' Woodger was another American volunteer who arrived in Malta in mid August, but he did not last long, as during an offensive sortie over Sicily on the 27th in Spitfire VC EP200/GL-T his fighter was hit by anti-aircraft fire and he force-landed to become a PoW (*G Cook*)

On 9 September Weaver was flying Spitfire VC BR112/X over Sicily when he engaged some C.202s, one of which he shot down. His Spitfire was then hit and he force-landed on a beach and was captured, although he later escaped. Weaver's aircraft had part of its camouflage overpainted in a dark blue shade, which was better suited to the local operating conditions (*via Wojtek Matusiak*)

Blitz on Malta, Flt Lt 'Rip' Jones attacked a Ju 88 head on off Malta but misjudged his approach, colliding with 3Z+AC of II./KG 77, flown by Knight's Cross holder Maj Paepcke. Both aircraft fell to their destruction, taking their crews with them. Jones' total had reached 7 and 2 shared destroyed prior to his demise.

The victory at El Alamein, and subsequent advance, and the Allied landings in French North Africa in the autumn of 1942 had the effect of transforming Malta's situation. Although life for both the population and the garrison was still grim, the threat of daily bombardment and possible invasion had passed, and it was now seen very much as a base for offensive operations.

In December, Flg Off John Lynch, who had two shared victories from his service in the UK, joined No 249 Sqn. North of the island of Lampedusa on the 11th he shot down a Bf 110 and claimed a Ju 52/3m as a probable to record his first victories while flying from Malta. Lynch shared in the destruction of a Ju 88 on 14 December, and three days later he was in one of six Spitfires escorting Beaufighters in an attack on Sicily. East of Cap Passero, the RAF fighters spotted two Ju 88s from LG 1 –

The most successful American Spitfire pilot by some margin was the CO of No 249 Sqn, Sqn Ldr John Lynch, who, amongst other claims, is also credited with scoring the 1000th victory for the Malta defences (*via Brian Cull*)

At the controls of Spitfire VC EP829 John Lynch was credited with 5.5 victories during April 1943. To the unit letters T-N his ground-crew added a small 'T', as the combination of this aircraft with Lynch in the cockpit was clearly dynamite! (*via Brian Cull*)

L1+RV, flown by Ofw Meyer, and Ltn Hahn's L1+DW. The fighters attacked immediately, with Lynch sharing in the destruction of both bombers, the first of which took him to ace status.

December also saw the departure of another of No 249 Sqn's Americans when the now Plt Off Vasseure Wynn left for the UK. There, he transferred to the USAAF and joined the 4th FG, with whom he reached ace status before becoming a PoW in April 1944.

With enemy attacks on Malta reduced, the Spitfires flew increasing numbers of offensive sorties, with now Flt Lt John Lynch claiming his first victory of 1943 on 7 February. A month later he became CO of the unit when Sqn Ldr M G McLeod was killed. Lynch's next victory came on 7 April when he shot down a Ju 88, and just after 0600 hrs on the 22nd, he led future RCAF ace Plt Off 'Hap' Kennedy on yet another low level sweep over Sicily. An hour later, off Riposto, they spotted a three-engined transport, which Kennedy destroyed. Around 0730 hrs, the pair intercepted three more transports low over the sea near the Lipari Islands, and in a one-sided fight all three Ju 52/3ms were claimed destroyed, two of them by Lynch.

The American found further success three days later when, early on the 25th, he attacked a Ca.313 over Axis shipping near Cap Milazzo. Initially attacking head-on, and then from astern, his fire hit the bomber hard, causing pieces to fly off before a fire broke out and it dived into the sea. Then, just after 0530 hrs on 28 April, Lynch found more success on another sweep off the Sicilian coast in what was becoming a personal vendetta against the enemy's air transport fleet.

Spotting a Ju 52/3m over the sea, Lynch fired a four-second burst, hitting it in the fuselage and causing the transport to trail a stream of vapour, before it dived into the water. Lynch's wingman attacked a second Junkers tri-motor, which the American ace then fired at head-on, before it too crashed into the sea, as he reported at the time. 'As soon as my Junkers crashed, I went off to see how my No 2 was doing. I found him attacking a Ju 52, and we finished it off together'. Lynch's first victim

With nine victories claimed over Tunisia and during the Pantelleria operation, 1Lt Sylvan Feld of the 4th FS was the most successful USAAF pilot to fly the Spitfire. Sadly, he was killed during the Normandy invasion the following year (*52nd FW*)

was identified as being the 1000th enemy aircraft downed by Malta-based aircraft, and for this success he received a congratulatory telegram.

Having shot down 5.5 enemy aircraft in April alone, and taken his total to six and seven shared destroyed, Lynch was also awarded an immediate, and well deserved, DFC. Then, with Axis air arms desperately trying to support trapped armies in North Africa, early on 10 May he intercepted a formation of transport aircraft evacuating Tunisia, shooting down a Ju 52/3m and two Cant Z.506Bs, as well as damaging an escorting Me 210. John Lynch received a bar to the DFC for this action.

The American ace continued to lead his squadron during the invasion of Sicily, mainly on escort work. During a Kittyhawk escort to Lentini on the evening of 13 July, three Fw 190s were spotted at 12,000 ft near Catania, and in a brief fight, Lynch shot one of them down to claim his final victory. This took his total to 17 destroyed (seven of them shared), which was the highest score by an American flying the Spitfire during the war. No 249 Sqn was retained for the defence of Malta, and soon afterwards Sqn Ldr J J Lynch transferred to the USAAF in the Mediterranean as a lieutenant colonel, although he saw no further action.

THE SICILY CAMPAIGN

After the conclusion of the campaign in North Africa, much to its frustration and chagrin, the 52nd FG remained at La Sebala on convoy work, which in turn meant very little contact with the enemy. However, in the late afternoon of 3 June, to the north of Cap Bon, Lt Sylvan Feld shot down an Fw 190. Then, in the early evening of the 6th, when patrolling about 12 miles west of the Italian-held island of Pantelleria, he had a successful combat with some Bf 109Gs, destroying one and damaging another. These final successes took Feld's tally to nine victories, making him the USAAF's most successful Spitfire pilot.

The 31st FG had moved to Korba on 15 May, and from there it began flying escort missions for medium bombers sent to attack Italian forces on Pantelleria. On 7 June, for example, the Spitfires escorted more than 500 bombers as they literally carpet-bombed the island, and two days later the destruction was even greater. During the late morning, in a cloudless sky over Pantelleria, 16 Spitfires from the 308th FS encountered an equal number of Axis fighters. In a one-sided fight five were downed, including four C.202s.

'Sid' Feld's Spitfire VC was ES276/WD-D, which was decorated with his impressive score (two kills being painted on the access door) when photographed in June 1943. The 4th FS also painted the pilot's name in a scripted style forward of the cockpit (*52nd FW*)

Among the successful pilots was 1Lt Royal N Baker (nicknamed 'the King'), who shot down a Bf 109G to set him on the path to becoming an ace with 15 and 3 shared victories – most of these were claimed flying F-86s over Korea in 1952-53.

On another mission flown later that same day, the 308th tangled with three dozen enemy fighters over an Allied convoy just offshore 24 hours before the landings on Pantelleria. In a savage free flowing fight, several pilots claimed, including 1Lt Alvin Callender, who would ultimately achieve four kills with the Spitfire.

On 10 June the 31st FG flew seven missions against Pantelleria and Lampedusa, as well as two defensive scrambles, claiming a dozen enemy aircraft destroyed. One went to the 309th FS's Capt Carl Payne, who wrote afterwards about the combat that had taken him to 'acedom';

'I climbed up from 800 ft, below and slightly behind one Macchi. The enemy fighter took evasive action, and I followed, firing short bursts whenever possible. The combat ended at 2000 ft when I fired a three-second burst of both cannon and machine gun fire from 200 to 150 yards. I saw strikes on the fuselage near the cockpit, and when the canopy was blown off, the pilot baled out.'

1Lt Dale Shafer got another to take his total to three, although he also reported being attacked by an American P-40, fortunately without harm. Also successful was 1Lt Charlie Fischette of the 307th FS, who claimed

One of the future aces who enjoyed success during the Pantelleria operation was 1Lt Dale Shafer of the 309th FS, who shot down a C.202 on the evening of 10 June during the same sortie that saw Capt Carl Payne become an ace. Shafer's excitement did not end there, as on the way home he was attacked by an over eager USAAF P-40 pilot (*via Brian Cull*)

Spitfire VC ES364/WD-F of the 4th FS crash-landed in Tunisia in mid 1943, possibly after operations in support of the landings on Pantelleria (*ww2 images*)

his third kill when he sent a Bf 109G to destruction, although he too was attacked by inexperienced P-40 pilots. Also on the score sheet from the 307th was 1Lt John White, who used his Spitfire IX to down an Fw 190 and a Bf 109G. Later, in the early evening, the 309th's Maj Frank Hill claimed his seventh, and last, victory when he destroyed a C.202.

The landings on Pantelleria went in on the 11th after the massive aerial bombardment, and during a sortie off the island in mid afternoon 1Lt Jerry Collinsworth, who was flying one of 18 307th FS Spitfire IXs protecting Allied shipping, became embroiled with a formation of Fw 190s some ten miles north of the invasion beaches. In the resulting fight, he shot one of them down to become the USAAF's latest ace – an achievement matched during the action by John White, who also got a Focke-Wulf for his fifth, and final, victory. The squadron gained a third ace during this mid afternoon combat, as Charlie Fischette shot down a brace of Bf 109Gs to take his total to five.

During an earlier patrol that day, Capt Royal Baker of the 308th, again in a Spitfire IX, shot down a Bf 109G. Also successful in claiming his sole victory during this mission was the 31st FG's well-respected CO, Lt Col Fred M Dean, flying his personal Spitfire bedecked with his initials 'FMD' in place of the squadron code letters. In two days Dean's group had destroyed 28 enemy fighters, and at the end of the month he led the 31st FG to the Maltese island of Gozo, where two aircraft crashed on landing on the rough strips.

Elsewhere, the 52nd FG's Spitfires found only desultory action from the group's bases in Tunisia, although on 1 July 1Lt John Carey became the 5th FS's first ace when his flight attacked three German fighters off Cap Bon and he shot down two Fw 190s. His wingman, Lt Charles O'Connor, described part of the encounter in a letter;

'Shortly after 0700 hrs a scramble was called, and 1Lt Carey and I roared off into the blue in a big cloud of dust, noise and excitement. We were vectored and climbed to 32,000 ft, where we began to patrol. We made a turn and I saw a flash of sunlight on someone's canopy, which turned out to be a "Jerry". 1Lt Carey was above me and quite a distance ahead due to the turn when all of a sudden two Fw 190s and a Me 109G came out of the sun above us. Apparently they had not seen us, for they made a 90-degree turn away. We "firewalled" everything, moved in behind them and started in. 1Lt Carey picked the nearest 190 and opened fire on him.'

A week later, Lt Robert Armstrong of the 4th FS shot down a Ju 88 off Bizerte, although he was also hit by return fire and baled out at almost 40,000 ft – and survived. This was his fourth victory but, frustratingly, his all-important fifth never came.

The maintenance board for the 308th FS in early September 1943 shows the mix of both Mks VB/Cs and VIIIs (and their engine numbers!) operated by the unit at the time. Also listed is the 31st FG commander's personal Mk VIII (*31st FW*)

The invasion of Sicily began with landings at Gela Bay early on 9 July 1943, the armada of landing ships being covered by a host of Allied fighters including the 31st FG's Spitfires, which flew continuous patrols from 0430 hrs to 2200 hrs, albeit with no action. However, things changed the next day when the group was credited with seven aircraft destroyed. One of the successful pilots was Carl Payne, flying a Spitfire VIII, and he described the action in his combat report;

'I was leading a section of Spitfire IXs on a patrol over the beachhead at Gela. At approximately 1615 hrs, while flying at 12,000 ft over Pazzollo, we saw an Fw 190 about 2000 ft above us. We climbed to engage, and as we came within range, he made a turn towards us and then entered a vertical dive. I followed and fired a three-second burst with cannons and machine guns at a range of 100 yards. I observed explosive shells striking in and behind the cockpit. The enemy aircraft immediately entered a violent spin from which it did not recover. As it crashed it exploded and burned.'

The following day another fell to Capt Jerry Collinsworth, giving him his sixth, and final, victory.

In preparation for the invasion of Sicily, the 31st FG moved to the Maltese island of Gozo. This aircraft of the 308th FS sits in a revetment at Luqa during August 1943 (*D H Newton via R L Ward*)

Parked on the Sicilian airfield of Licata shortly after the invasion in July 1943, Spitfire VC ES317/MX-F of the 307th FS was the regular aircraft of 1Lt Ron Brown (*H Levy via Jerry Scutts*)

By the time the 31st FG reached Sicily, its commander, Lt Col Fred M Dean, was flying Spitfire IX EN329/FM-D, which he passed on to Lt Col Frank Hill when he relinquished command of the group to him (*F Hill via W Matusiak*)

On the 13th the 31st FG moved into a strip at Ponte Olivo, just inland from the invasion beaches. Following the recent promotion of Lt Col Dean, Maj Frank Hill was elevated to replace him as the group commander, and Carl Payne replaced Hill as CO of the 309th FS.

After just ten days at Ponte Olivo, the group moved west along the coast to Agrigento, from where it would be tasked with covering Allied troops approaching the city of Palermo. Following the capture of the Sicilian capital, the 307th FS moved into its local airfield on 27 July. The day after the move, Lts Trafton and Muchler had a bizarre engagement with a pair of Bf 109Gs after being bounced. The Axis fighters continued diving down after attacking the USAAF aircraft, hotly pursued by the Americans in their Spitfire VIIIs. The latter machines soon gained on the Germans, who simply steepened their dives and flew straight into the sea! The incident was reported but neither pilot was allowed to make a claim.

31st FG CO Lt Col Frank Hill leans on his final mount, probably at Milazzo, in Sicily. Spitfire VIII JF452/FA-H which carried his initials, was passed onto his successor, Col Charles McCorkle (*F Hill via C F Shores*)

The only American ace of Korean ancestry was 1Lt Fred Ohr of the 2nd FS, who flew high level protection patrols from Sicily, having claimed his only Spitfire victory in April 1943. He became an ace when he scored five victories flying the P-51 in mid 1944 (*via Norman Franks*)

Spitfire IX QP-N of the 2nd FS was flown on occasion from Palermo by future ace 1Lt Fred Ohr during August 1943 (*J Fawcett via Dr Alfred Price*)

Much to the relief of its pilots, the end of July also saw part of the 52nd FG move across the Mediterranean with the arrival of the 2nd and 4th FSs at Bocca di Falco, near Palermo. They immediately began patrolling the harbour, although the 5th FS remained in Tunisia, and on 12 August claimed the last USAAF Spitfire victory in North Africa when an Fw 190 was shot down off Bizerte. The squadron moved to Bo Rizzo, near Trapani, soon afterwards.

There had been regular nocturnal intrusions by the enemy over Sicily since the invasion, and in an effort to counter these raids Capt Norman McDonald of the 2nd FS decided to try some nightflying. Just before dawn on 1 August he got airborne in a standard Spitfire IX, with 1Lt Dave Macmillan as his wingman. After a period of monotony, and with dawn breaking, something was seen, as McDonald later recounted;

'Eureka! Dead ahead, two bombers about 1000 ft above us. Now another period of apprehension. Full throttle but not catching up very fast at all. Afraid to climb and lose precious speed. "Dave, they are Dorniers". These are biggies – I've never been on the tail of one of these before. Hey, they are losing altitude! They are separating. Are we still over the sea? They haven't seen us, that's for sure. I'll take the one on the left. Good luck! In range, but really would like to get closer. Damned Dorniers are faster than I thought! Better give him a good long burst in the belly before he sees me and starts shooting. Right on target! Another burst gets the right engine. A third and final burst to the belly and the left engine – no more cannon ammo now. He's headed down, both engines flaming and pouring black smoke.'

McDonald's final Spitfire victim went into the sea off the volcanic island of Stromboli, and his wingman got the second Dornier.

Enemy air activity during daylight hours had by now significantly decreased, although on 8 August, while covering a landing at Cap Orlando, 31st FG pilots intercepted an attack by around 20 German fighter-bombers. The dozen Spitfires (half of them superb Mk VIIIs) quickly downed three Fw 190s and damaged a fourth. One of the successful pilots was 2Lt Richard Hurd, who thus began his path to 'acedom', while Royal Baker damaged another. The latter pilot subsequently shot down an Fw 190 in the same area three days later for his final Spitfire victory.

Spitfire VC JK777/QP-Z of the 2nd FS joined the squadron in July 1943, and it is seen here at Bocca di Falco, from where the squadron protected the port of Palermo. The aircraft was regularly flown on such patrols during August and September by future ace 2Lt 'Dixie 'Alexander (*R L Alexander via Norman Franks*)

With its RAF wing and fin markings still in place, 4th FS Spitfire VC JG878/WD-V undergoes engine runs after reassembly, probably at Bocca di Falco, in Sicily. The squadron was engaged in coastal escort operations over the Mediterranean at the time (*via Wojtek Matusiak*)

Enemy forces had been steadily evacuating across the Straits of Messina to mainland Italy during the first two weeks of August, and the last German troops left Messina on the night of the 16th, abandoning their Italian allies and tons of materiel. And with the fall of Messina the campaign in Sicily was effectively ended. Allied forces now turned their attention to Italy.

For the 52nd FG, however, there was little sign of the Luftwaffe, much to everyone's frustration, and so they continued on local defensive patrols. In mid-August an old Spitfire hand had joined the 2nd FS when 2Lt 'Dixie' Alexander, having been released from a period of internment in Portugal, renewed his acquaintance with the Supermarine fighter.

CORSICAN SOJOURN

British and Commonwealth forces moved into Italy via the Straits of Messina on 3 September, and once again the action passed the 52nd FG by. Indeed, during September the group did not fly a single combat mission! The monotonous grind of standby and convoy escort, often in poor weather, seemed to be its lot. However, on 4 October, French and Italian troops that had landed in Corsica captured the capital, Bastia, and at the beginning of December the 52nd moved to the island, with the 4th FS going to Calvi and the 2nd and 5th FSs to Borgo. There, they began to convert to fighter-bomber duties, with the 2nd flying its first mission from Corsica on 5 October – a shipping reconnaissance off the coast of Italy. Sweeps along the Italian coast attacking ground targets then became the daily routine, although these sorties were routinely interrupted by the unpredictable weather, and the heavy rains did not improve conditions on the ground either.

After a long barren run the 52nd FG encountered the enemy in the air once again when, in the mid morning of 7 December, a pair of Spitfires from the 4th FS were scrambled after an intruder and eventually shot down an Me 210 – the group's first victory for more than three months. The following day, Capt Lee M Trowbridge of the 4th FS had a narrow escape during a tactical reconnaissance mission over southern France. His return to Calvi was witnessed by a pilot of a co-located RAF squadron, who recalled, 'While attacking a locomotive on the way home, he flew so low he hit a flagpole, leaving a 15-ft length of pole embedded in his wing. The flagpole impacted very close to the starboard side of the fuselage. He success-fully belly landed back at base, and the pole was kept as a Mess decoration'.

Shortly after this incident, Trowbridge was made squadron CO, and he subsequently claimed two victories in January 1944 to take his total to 2.5 kills.

During yet another reconnaissance mission off the coast of southern France a few days before Christmas, Capt Kelly attacked an E-boat, which he left low in the water on fire.

With the 2nd FS's Spitfire VBs now modified to carry a pair of 250-lb bombs beneath their wings, unit CO Maj Robert Levine and Lt Fuller flew the squadron's first dive-bombing mission on 28 December. The following day, 'Dixie' Alexander, along with fellow future ace 2Lt Dan Zoerb, went dive-bombing for the first time, attacking Viareggio harbour. Alexander clearly rated his wingman Zoerb, commenting that he 'had all the flying abilities you could ask for. He was a good tactician, and missed nothing. He had excellent eyes, coordination and the ability to act on a moment's notice in any situation. He was quiet and reserved, but resourceful and adamant in a controversy'.

Both men would need all their flying skill, and a fair slice of luck, to survive the dive-bombing mission now thrust upon the 52nd FG, for as the 2nd FS quickly found out, it was a hazardous occupation that soon inflicted a growing number of casualties on the unit. However, this tactical switch meant that the group would now become more involved in the hard slog of the Italian campaign.

After service with the RAF, 2Lt 'Dixie' Alexander transferred to the USAAF and joined the 2nd FS. He enjoyed considerable success flying the Spitfire with this unit until it re-equipped with P-51s, on which he became an ace in 1944 (*R L Alexander via Norman Franks*)

COLOUR PLATES

1
Spitfire IIA P7308/XR-D of Plt Off W R Dunn, No 71 'Eagle' Sqn, North Weald, 27 August 1941

2
Spitfire VB AB908/XR-Y of Plt Off C W McColpin, No 71 'Eagle' Sqn, North Weald, September-October 1941

3
Spitfire VB BL287/XR-C of Plt Off L Nomis, No 71 'Eagle' Sqn, Martlesham Heath, 17 April 1942

4
Spitfire VB BL753/YO-H of Plt Off D J W Blakeslee, No 401 Sqn RCAF, Gravesend, April-May 1942

5
Spitfire VB EN918/AV-X of Flt Lt S R Edner, No 121 'Eagle' Sqn, Southend, July-August 1942

6
Spitfire VB BM635/WZ-Y of 2Lt D E Shafer Jr, 309th FS/31st FG, High Ercall, 29 June 1942

7
Spitfire VB (serial overpainted)/MX-A of 2Lt J H White, 307th FS/31st FG, Westhampnett, 19 August 1942

8
Spitfire VB EP179/WZ-A of Maj H R Thyng, 309th FS/31st FG, Westhampnett, 22 September 1942

9
Spitfire VB EN853/AV-D of Maj W J Daley, 335th FS/4th FG, Debden, October 1942

10
Spitfire VB BM510/XR-A of Maj G A Daymond, 334th FS/4th FG, Debden, October 1942

11
Spitfire VB BL722/MD-B of Lt J A Goodson, 336th FS/4th FG, Debden, October 1942

12
Spitfire VB BL255/MD-T of Lt D S Gentile, 336th FS/4th FG, Debden, November 1942

13
Spitfire VB BL545/MD-L of Capt O H Coen, 336th FS/4th FG, Debden, 22 January 1943

14
Spitfire VB BL449(?)/CG-P of Lt Col C G Peterson, 4th FG, Debden, December 1942-January 1943

15
Spitfire IX BS513/PK-Z of Capt F S Gabreski, No 315 'Deblinski' Sqn, Northolt, January-February 1943

16
Spitfire VC BR112/X of Plt Off C Weaver RCAF, No 185 Sqn, Ta Kali, Malta, 9 September 1942

17
Spitfire VC BR390/ZX-N of Flt Sgt MacA Powers, No 145 Sqn, LG 173, Egypt, 2 November 1942

18
Spitfire VC ES252/ZX-E of Sqn Ldr L C Wade, No 145 Sqn, Bu Grara, Tunisia, March 1943

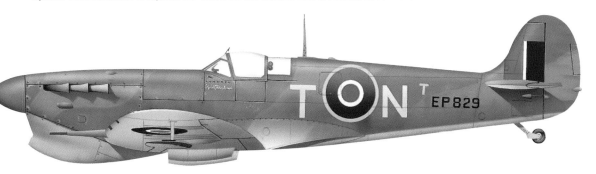

19
Spitfire VC EP829/T-N of Sqn Ldr J J Lynch, No 249 Sqn, Qrendi, Malta, April 1943

20
Spitfire VC ER570/WD-Q of Maj R Levine, 4th FS/52nd FG, La Sers, Tunisia, April 1943

21
Spitfire IX EN447/WD-L of Lt V N Cabas, 4th FS/52nd FG, Le Sers, Tunisia, 19 April 1943

22
Spitfire VC (serial overpainted)/MX-Y of Lt J D Collinsworth, 307th FS/31st FG, La Sers, Tunisia, 6 May 1943

23
Spitfire VC ER187/WZ-C of Maj F A Hill, 309th FS/31st FG, La Sers, Tunisia, 6 May 1943

24
Spitfire VC ES276/WD-D of 1Lt S Feld, 4th FS/52nd FG, La Sebala, Tunisia, June 1943

25
Spitfire IX (serial overpainted)/QP-N of Lt F Ohr, 2nd FS/52nd FG, Palermo, Sicily, August 1943

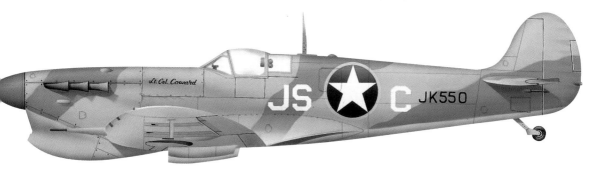

26
Spitfire VC JK550/JS-C of Lt Col J S Coward, 52nd FG, Palermo, Sicily, August 1943

27
Spitfire VC JK777/QP-Z of 1Lt R L Alexander, 2nd FS/52nd FG, Bocca di Falco, Sicily, August-September 1943

28
Spitfire VIII JF452/FA-H of Col F A Hill, 31st FG, Termini and Milazzo, Sicily, September 1943

29
Spitfire VC (serial overpainted)/WZ-S of 1Lt G G Loving, 309th FS/31st FG, Pomigliano, Italy, December 1943

30
Spitfire VIII JF452/CM-M of Col C M McCorkle, 31st FG, Castel Volturno, Italy, January-February 1944

31
Spitfire VIII (serial overpainted)/HL-X of 1Lt L P Molland, 308th FS/31st FG, Castel Volturno, Italy, February 1944

32

Spitfire XVI TB752/KH-Z of Sqn Ldr H P M Zary RCAF, No 403 Sqn RCAF, B114 Diepholz, Germany, 21 April 1945

ITALY –
THE HARD YARDS

After the successful ejection of the enemy from Sicily, the Allies swiftly moved to establish their presence on mainland Europe with the invasion of Italy on 3 September. Within days of the British 8th Army kicking off the campaign by crossing the Straits of Messina, the 31st FG flew into Milazzo, to the west of Messina. From here, it would see considerable action. Then, on the 9th, the US 5th Army landed at Salerno, to the south of Naples. However, for much of the next two months pilots of the 52nd FG would sit frustrated in Sicily.

Leading the 31st FG's 309th FS during the early phases of the Italy campaign was ace Maj Carl Payne, and the day after the Allied landings, he described some of the aerial activity he saw over Salerno;

'I sighted a formation of 18 Me 109s that were preparing to bomb the beach. I attacked the formation, causing them to jettison their bombs and split up. I then chased two of the enemy fighters, and was able to close to a range of 300 yards, at which point I opened fire with cannons and machine guns. I saw my tracers hitting the enemy aircraft as he half-rolled from 18,000 ft down to the deck – I followed, firing one-second bursts whenever possible. I was not able to close to a range of less than 300 yards at any time. I continued the chase on the deck for three minutes, firing all my ammunition. I broke off combat when I thought it advisable not to go deeper into enemy territory.'

Payne's last claim over Europe was, therefore, a damaged, and during the same engagement Capt Dale Shafer went one better and shot down an Fw 190 for his fourth, and final, Spitfire victory.

Ten days later, the 31st FG moved onto the European mainland when its Spitfires flew across to Montecorvino, a few miles south of Salerno.

Over Salerno on the day the 5th Army invaded southern Italy (9 September 1943), 1Lt Carroll Pryblo was hit by 'friendly' anti-aircraft fire and forced to crash-land his Spitfire VC. He survived the experience and eventually mustered three victories, two of which were claimed in Spitfires (*via Wojtek Matusiak*)

Spitfire IX MH894/WZ-JJ, named
Lady Ellen III, was the regular
aircraft of 1Lt John Fawcett of
the 309th FS, and it wore the RAF
grey/green/grey temperate
camouflage scheme (*J Fawcett
via ww2images*)

For the first time since the previous February, the group's personnel now enjoyed permanent accommodation, rather than living in tents. Part of Twelfth Air Support Command, the group was tasked with performing bomber escort and close support missions for ground forces, with the latter role meaning that it was generally based close to the frontline.

Among the new pilots to join the group upon its move to Italy was 2Lt John Fawcett, who was much impressed by his CO;

'The skipper of the 309th FS was young, competent, battle-tested Carl Payne – probably the best fighter pilot I ever met. He had been with the squadron since it left England, and had five or six victories to his credit, all of them gotten the hard way in the Africa campaign. His successor was Capt Garth Jared, whose easy-going gift of leadership was soon tested in combat. He set an example for all of us in quality of conduct, courage and firm friendship.'

Command of the 31st FG also changed in the autumn of 1943 when the much respected Lt Col Frank Hill was replaced by future 11-victory ace Col Charles M McCorkle. The latter soon made his mark when he claimed his first kill (an Me 210) in the late afternoon of 30 September. However, the bad weather in October then restricted operations somewhat, and on the 14th the 31st FG moved to Pomigliano, just inland from Naples at the foot of Mount Vesuvius – an active volcano!

Spitfire VIII JF400 undergoes
acceptance tests before joining
the 308th FS on operations over
southern Italy (*R S G Mackay*)

The RAF Spitfire squadrons in Italy were also heavily involved in the action during this period, with Sqn Ldr Lance Wade's No 145 Sqn being based at Gioia del Colle, to the north of Taranto. On 2 October Wade was leading a patrol of eight Spitfire VIIIs when he sighted a formation of Fw 190 fighter-bombers from III./SG 4 at 12,000 ft off Pemna Point, on the Italian coast near Termoli. Wade led his formation in a climb to engage the enemy, positioning his charges to approach from behind and below. He subsequently wrote in his combat report, 'After gaining this position, and approaching unseen to within 200 yards, I destroyed the rearmost Fw 190 with a burst of cannon fire. I then moved behind the next fighter, and with another burst sent the enemy plunging earthward'.

One of Wade's victims was Ofw Pellender, and these last two kills took his final total to 25 (two of them shared), thus making him the leading Allied fighter pilot in the Mediterranean at that time. Ten of his victories had been claimed in Spitfires.

No 145 Sqn's Spitfire VIIIs were very active in support of the 8th Army as it pushed north from Messina. One of the aircraft involved was JF503/ZX-W, which carries the squadron badge on its fin. It is seen here undergoing maintenance in the open at Marchianise (*via J D R Rawlings*)

The most successful American fighter pilot to fly exclusively with the RAF was No 145 Sqn's CO, Sqn Ldr Lance Wade, who at the time of his death had 22 and 2 shared victories (ten in Spitfires) to his credit (*via Wojtek Matusiak*)

67

Lance Wade's successor as CO of No 145 Sqn was another successful American, Sqn Ldr 'Sandy' Kallio, whose tour was cut short by a broken leg (*Canadian Forces*)

On return to duty, Kallio assumed command of No 417 Sqn, which flew Spitfire VIIIs – including JF627/AN-M, fitted with extended high altitude wingtips (*Canadian Forces*)

In November the 31st FG found increasing evidence of stiffening Luftwaffe resistance, its pilots having claimed a number of successes against four losses. On the 13th, the 307th FS's 1Lt Tucker and his CO, Capt Virgil Fields, each destroyed a Bf 109G. Also busy was No 145 Sqn's Lance Wade, who, with his wingman, over San Severo on the 3rd engaged a larger formation of Fw 190s and claimed three damaged in a hectic fight. He did not have time to see the results of his frenzied attacks, although Uffz Walz was in fact lost. These were the charismatic Texan's final claims, for he was promoted soon afterwards and replaced by fellow American Sqn Ldr 'Sandy' Kallio from Michigan, who already had three destroyed to his name.

On 2 December Kallio opened his account with his new unit by claiming a Bf 109G probably destroyed near Palena when flying Spitfire VIII JF472. He used this aircraft again to damage an Fw 190 near Palena on the 30th of the month. Then, on 18 February 1944, Kallio shot down an Fw 190 to claim his last victory, but the following day he broke his leg and was grounded. Fit once again by June, 'Sandy' Kallio returned to action as CO of Spitfire-equipped No 417 Sqn, but by then the Luftwaffe was largely a spent force in Italy, and so his fifth victory never came. Nevertheless, he ended his very successful tour with a DSO to his name.

Tragically, 'Wildcat' Wade would be killed in a flying accident at Amendola after visiting his old unit early in the New Year. The demise of the most successful American Spitfire pilot was witnessed by Paul Carll, a pilot with the 57th FG's 64th FS;

'It occurred on Wednesday, 12 January 1944 at about 1500 hrs. Lance was flying a Spitfire V, and in his role as CO of the RAF's No 239 Wing, he had came over to visit our CO, Lt Col Archie Knight. He arrived at about 1400 hrs. They had their meeting, which lasted for about an hour, and Lance prepared to leave. Our strip lay east to west. The wind was from the east, and Lance took off from west to east. The west end of the runway was directly south of our tent.

'I watched him take-off, and as soon as he got off the ground and picked up his wheels, he did a slow roll. He remained low and did a 180-degree left hand turn. He came back parallel to the runway, between our tent and the runway, and started another slow roll. He fell out of this one right before my eyes. His left wing hit the ground and the aeroplane crashed and burned furiously. Lance had no chance. The Spitfire V he was flying

was used as a utility aeroplane by the Headquarters flight of No 239 Wing, whilst its frontline units were primarily operational with newer model Spitfires. Speculation was that Lance had not made allowance for the underpowered Mk V. There was no room for error when performing a manoeuvre like that.'

In spite of the onset of the winter weather, which made flying more hazardous and life on the ground more miserable, the 31st FG continued operations, and had occasional brushes with the enemy. During a patrol of the Cassino area by six Spitfires of the 308th on 7 December, a dozen enemy fighters were encountered. In the action that followed, it was thought that half the enemy group was destroyed, with a Bf 109G and an Fw 190 falling to the guns of 1Lt Mick Ainley. He also claimed another Messerschmitt fighter as a probable to begin his journey to ace status. Also gaining a double victory was his CO, Maj Garth Jared, with the two remaining kills being credited to Capt Barr and 1Lt Blumenstock.

There were several more encounters in the middle of the month, with one of the successful pilots being future ace Capt Virgil Fields, who gained his third victory.

ANZIO CAULDRON

The 31st FG was heavily engaged with the Luftwaffe through the early part of January 1944, and group CO Col Charles McCorkle showed the way when, over Venafro in mid-afternoon on the 3rd, he brought down an Fw 190. Three days later, in his personally marked Spitfire VIII, he shot down another Focke-Wulf to the north of Froisinone. On the 16th there was further action, the group records stating that 'The 308th, on a bomb line patrol in a mixed formation of eight Mk VIIIs and six Mk Vs, ran smack into 24 mixed Me 109s and Fw 190s headed for Venafro. Lt Brunasky and Lt Molland divided an Me-109 between them, literally'. For 24-year-old North Dakotan Leland Molland in one of the Spitfire VIIIs, it was his first step to 'acedom'.

The 52nd FG, meanwhile, continued its dive-bombing operations, achieving some outstanding results against Axis shipping, railways and fixed installations. On the 10 January, for example, 'Dixie' Alexander and Dan Zoerb attacked a 700-ton F-boat (fleet escort, or frigate), scoring some near misses. Future 2nd FS 14-kill ace 1Lt Bob Curtis outlined the hazards of such work when recalling a mission he flew on 18 January;

'"Dixie" led a flight of four aeroplanes. The target was protected by three or four flak boats. When we got near the target, we climbed to about 3000 ft in order to get the minimum altitude necessary for a dive-bombing attack. During the climb, the flak boats were filling the air with tracers – a sight that I remember vividly to this day. "Dixie" was first and I was second.

One of the up and coming pilots in the 2nd FS in 1944 was 1Lt Bob Curtis, who flew some of the unit's first fighter-bomber sorties. He later rose to command the squadron, and become a 14-victory ace, the first of which he scored in the Spitfire in mid-February 1944 (*R C Curtis via Norman Franks*)

We were all a bit too closely spaced for a judicious attack. During my dive, I saw "Dixie's" bombs burst alongside the ship – a perfect near miss, which is best because it blows in the side of the ship. My bombs hit directly on the deck and Haskins said that he thought the debris that came up would blow him out of the sky.'

Although Axis forces in the MTO were very much on the back foot, they still had plenty of fight left in them. Indeed, in January 1944 alone, the 31st and 52nd FGs lost no fewer than 16 Spitfires in combat.

18 January also saw the 31st FG begin its move to the steel mat-covered strip at Castel Volturno, at the mouth of the Volturno River. Now closer to the enemy, the group was well positioned to cover the landings at Anzio and Nettuno, to the southwest of Rome. Just two days after the move, the 308th FS commenced operations with an early morning patrol over the beachhead. Initially, things were quiet, then as part of its third sweep, the unit escorted medium bombers, which attracted the attention of two dozen enemy fighters. 2Lt Tommy Molland destroyed a Bf 109G whilst defending the bombers, and went on to claim his third success in five days just after midday on the 21st.

The 307th FS flew only two missions on the 20th, although the unit found some success, as the group diary recorded;

'At 1240 hrs, eight Spitfires took off as target cover for 24 A-20s sent to blast Pontecorvo. As the bombers crossed the coastline on their run-in to the target, they were intercepted by 15 enemy fighters, which had approached from the direction of Gaeta. Maj Fields and Lt Vaughn, flying above them as "Outlaw" section, contacted the squadron to report the situation, and then turned into the enemy. There was no doubt that the enemy fighters were being vectored to the bombers, but when Maj Fields and Lt Vaughn charged into them, the enemy formation broke and ran! Fields and Vaughn gave chase after three German fighters bunched together heading northwest in their dive. Maj Fields fired at the last of these, getting numerous hits and tail feathers before the three Axis fighters plunged into clouds.'

Fields, who had already claimed four victories flying Spitfires, was frustrated, and could only claim a damaged, but Vaughn was credited with one destroyed, while two other pilots shared in the destruction of a second enemy fighter.

On 22 January the 5th Army, led by Gen Mark Clark, began landing at Anzio, and so greater enemy air activity was anticipated in spite of the very hazy weather that resulted in poor visibility.

2Lt 'Dixie' Alexander's Spitfire VC QP-A that he flew from Borgo, Corsica, from late 1943 wore a spectacular sharksmouth marking. He recorded its demise in his logbook on 21 January 1944. 'Unhappy day – fini QP-A. Recco Piombino to La Spezia. Skip-bombed electric plant, shot up Macchi 200, two trucks, cleaned out one gun post. Was hit by three cannon bursts and lots of machine gun. Flaps gone, one elevator, one wingtip, crashed base, Category C. Bumped head, sore arm and leg' (R L Alexander via Norman Franks)

Col Charles McCorkle continued his run of success when, during a dusk patrol over the Anzio beachhead, he shot down a Bf 109G. He also related an incident that occurred over the invasion beaches;

'Maj Thorsen, who was one of my squadron commanders, was shot down over the Anzio beachhead. He had to force land on the beachhead, and as he was going down with his engine puffing smoke and pouring oil, and looking for a place to set down, for some reason he didn't want to bale out. An ME-109 pulled up alongside him, skidded down to his speed, or approximately that, in sort of a slip and saw that he was going to have to land. The German then saluted Thorsen and flew away, rather than shooting at him. This was the last piece of chivalry I ever heard of in air combat.'

The 52nd FG pilots returned to their air combat roots on 23 January when, in the late afternoon, a pair of 2nd FS Spitfires shot down a Ju 88, and a little while later, when on a dive-bombing sortie, four Spitfires spotted a large raid inbound to Anzio and attacked, downing six bombers. One fell to 1Lt Arthur Johnson Jr, who thus claimed his first victory – he became an ace later in the year when flying Mustangs. Johnson noted in his report;

'As our flight approached the Italian coast near Viareggio, we sighted more than 50 bombers, and two He 177s below us, headed for the Anzio-Nettuno beachhead. We jettisoned our bombs over the water and went after some He 111s. At this point, the two He 177s headed inland. I manoeuvred onto the tail of an He 111. After I fired several bursts it blew up, and I flew through the debris. I then got onto the tail of another He 111 and gave it a couple of bursts, hitting the right engine. At this time I looked up and saw a flight of Me 210s above, so I broke off and headed for home.'

The following day, a joint patrol of 2nd and 5th FS aircraft had a running fight with six Do 217s, two of which fell to the Spitfires' guns. 'Art' Johnson was again successful;

'I was flying wingman to Schellhase in a flight of six Spitfires when we encountered six low-flying Do 217s overland near Viareggio. We attacked while some of the others remained above as cover. I followed Schellhase as he attacked a bomber from the rear. As we neared the bomber, Schellhase peeled up and to the right. That was the last I saw of him, but heard later that he had crashed. We were only a few hundred feet off the ground.

'My left cannon was not working, so every time I fired a burst, my aeroplane would yaw to the right. I then began aiming at the left engine, and would fire until the yawing brought the strikes along the bomber to its right engine. After about three of these exercises, the bomber plowed into the ground. Probably the yawing of my aeroplane due to the jammed cannon saved me from being hit by return fire.'

That same day, future ace 1Lt Bob Curtis damaged a Ju 88 on the ground near Pisa, as did another pilot who would reach 'acedom' on the Mustang, 2Lt Barry Lawler.

The enemy reaction to the landings was fierce, and there was heavy fighting on and over the beachhead. On the 26th, the 307th and 308th FSs escorted a large formation of A-20s sent to bomb targets around Cisterna, but on their return to base the Spitfire pilots were ordered to land at

Twenty-one-year-old 2Lt 'Art' Johnson claimed the first two of his 8.5 victories when flying Spitfires with the 2nd FS on consecutive days in late January 1944 during sweeps over northwestern Italy (*via Norman Franks*)

a nearby strip that they discovered was under attack from about a dozen Bf 109s and Fw 190s! Leading the formation in a Spitfire IX, Maj Virgil Fields got on the tail of an Fw 190 and fired an accurate burst, whereupon the pilot promptly baled out to give the 307th FS CO his fifth victory.

Two days later, during a dawn patrol over the Anzio beachhead, Fields' Spitfire was hit, and badly damaged, by a P-40, but on his next mission he shot down another Fw 190 to claim his final success.

The 52nd FG continued its offensive work, and during an F-boat sweep on 27 January, 2Lt James 'Junior' Adams spotted a Do 24 flying-boat as it was landing. He was able to inflict damage on the Dornier, as he described post-mission in his combat report;

2Lt 'Junior' Adams of the 2nd FS claimed a total of 4.5 victories, including one with the Spitfire. He took part in many of the squadron's roving fighter-bomber patrols off the west coast of Italy in early 1944, and during one such mission he attacked a large Do 24 flying-boat as it alighted (*J A Adams via Norman Franks*)

'Got a squirt at a Do 24 at Spezia. This flying-boat was on its final approach to the harbour when I jumped it, line astern. I was too close, and fishtailed to bracket it with my fire. Saw some hits, but it landed and groundlooped (waterlooped?!). Had to leave in a hurry, as some people on the ground were very unfriendly.'

A few days later 1Lt William J Roberts destroyed one of these large aircraft over the Gulf of Spezia for the first of his two victories.

The 52nd FG also remained active from Corsica, mounting more than a thousand sorties during February – the 2nd and 5th FSs were based at Borgo, on the east coast, while the 4th remained at Calvi, on the west coast. These ground attack missions were hazardous, and losses to deadly light flak were considerable, but regular encounters with the Luftwaffe also meant a steady stream of claims too.

Triumphs and tragedy

To provide even closer cover, on 1 February the 307th FS was moved forward to a small strip at Nettuno, just to the south of Anzio, where the squadron found itself under constant artillery fire. The unit was eventually withdrawn after just two weeks, although not before enemy shelling had destroyed four Spitfires on the ground.

During a patrol over Anzio on 6 February, Charles McCorkle, again in his personal Spitfire VIII, claimed another Bf 109G. This victory took him to 'acedom', as he recalled many years later;

'I had chased a German to the deck in a 109, and he was hit many times and was smoking. The enemy fighter was, very slowly, being overtaken by me, and I was just about out of ammunition, too, when suddenly he rocked his wings, in the old school signal of saying "Okay, you win, I've had enough", and he pulled straight up in the air to a thousand feet or so, pushed over, and baled out. I think he was saying, "Okay, no need to shoot any more, I'm baling out".'

This was McCorkle's final success in the British fighter, although he would subsequently claim six more victories after his group converted to the P-51.

This day was also marked by a great tragedy for the 31st FG, however, as a lone Bf 109G bounced the Spitfire flown by 307th FS CO Maj Virgil Fields and set it on fire with its first burst. Spitfire IX ER130 crashed in flames near Anzio, killing the ace. The group diarist wrote;

'The patrol returned to base loose, scattered and badly shaken by the loss of their commanding officer. The entire squadron was stunned and mute at the death of Maj Fields. Not only was he greatly liked and admired by everyone, of every rank, but he was also a great friend, a leader and a fighter. Now he was gone. It was beyond all comprehension.'

That same day, 6 February, the 2nd FS found some welcome air action near Malignano airfield, as 1Lt 'Dixie' Alexander recounted in his combat report;

'I was leading an eight-man sweep of the Italian mainland, between Leghorn and Florence, when I observed two aircraft at "nine o'clock below" on the deck. As I called them in and turned down to attack, I saw several more aircraft on the deck, which I called in as well. I came up on two aircraft, bypassed the first – an HS 123 – and chose to attack an Fl 156 Storch. The Storch did not have a lot of room to turn, but used every bit that he could, and my first two bursts were in the back of him. My third burst was made with all the deflection I thought I could possibly need, and hit him in the tail section. The whole tail section came off, and he made a couple of little spirals into the ground.

'I pulled back upstairs to see what was going on, and it was like a great contest of hare and hounds scurrying about. It was a wonder that the entire flight was not wiped out by running into each other, or into the mountains on either side. By the end of the fight, I had destroyed an Fl 156 Storch, Lt Schneider an HS 126, Flt Off McGraw an HS 123 and Lt Taff of the Fifth Squadron an HS 123.'

When chided by colleagues about his victim, 'Dixie' replied, 'Who knows? He might have grown up to be a Me 109 pilot!' The following day, the 4th ran into some Hs 126s towing gliders, and shot down four of them – the successful pilots were 2Lt Bishop and 1Lts McCampbell, Burnett and Canning. The last two also claimed a glider each, but Canning suffered an engine failure and took to his parachute to become a 'guest' of the enemy. Later in the day, future Mustang ace 'Junior' Adams of the 2nd FS achieved his one and only Spitfire kill when, during a scramble off Pointe Palazzo, he downed an Me 410. After such a long period of lean pickings, these two days seemed like largesse indeed for the 52nd's pilots.

In improving weather, 31st FG units were active too, as early on the 7th the 309th FS sent a dozen aircraft on a patrol over Anzio at about 0715 hrs. About an hour later, they spotted a large formation of enemy fighters, and the Spitfires immediately engaged them. Lt Benzing shot an Fw 190 down, but his wingman was lost, while 1Lt Ray Harmeyer hit another Fw 190 at 10,000 ft and it fell away, but to his chagrin it recovered just above the ground and headed away to the north. Another of the 309th FS's future stars, Lt Richard Faxon, was also frustrated when, having pursued another Focke-Wulf as far as Rome, it escaped. Others were also

engaged, but only one destroyed and two damaged were claimed for several American losses.

Later in the morning ten more of the 309th's Spitfires escorted a B-26 raid, and near Bracciano the formation was attacked by 14 enemy fighters. Both Lts Souch and Loving fired at a Bf 109G, as George Loving described in his memoirs;

'I was flying wing to Charlie Souch, who was "Hobnail Red Leader". As he started out from our perch 4000 ft above the bombers, I shoved my throttle forward and slid in a little closer. We headed down steeply on a path that would intercept the Me-109s before they reached a firing position. Souch began firing before we were within range, spewing a stream of 0.30-calibre tracers and 20 mm shells ahead of the lead aircraft. I chimed in with a burst of fire. Moments later I saw an explosion on the port wing of the Luftwaffe leader, who broke off his attack on the bombers and turned toward us. As we passed through the Me-109 formation, where aircraft were careering in all directions, I got off a good volley without observing any hits. Minutes later "Hobnail Blue" section fended off a second wave of attackers. That ended the German challenge. Souch claimed one damaged.

'Years later I learned that Souch was credited with a half victory, probably on the basis of gun camera film, with the other half credit going to an unnamed pilot – I may have been that unnamed pilot.'

If that was so, then George Loving's first success was indeed on the Spitfire – he later became a five-kill ace during the summer flying P-51Bs.

The improvement in the weather meant an increase in enemy raids, and as dusk fell on 12 February

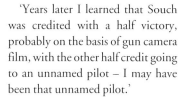

more than 40 Ju 88s and Do 217s bombed Anzio, starting a number of fires, but for some reason the 307th's Spitfires were not scrambled! The following lunchtime, a 309th FS beachhead patrol ran into some Fw 190s, and 1Lt Ray Harmeyer from New Orleans destroyed two of them, thus starting him on his path to 'acedom', as described by his element leader, 1Lt John Fawcett;

'He was my wingman on the morning of 13 February over Anzio when two Fw 190s, flying in line abreast, cruised right under us a thousand feet below as though they were on a sightseeing flight! I called the break and we rolled upside down and went storming down behind them. In the process, Harmeyer, who was on my left, got about a hundred yards or so ahead of me. As we got close, he turned slightly to the right in front of me and got off a snap shot at the right hand target, which immediately blew up in a great cloud of black smoke, flame and scrap aluminum, which it seemed to me then that I flew right through!

'Harmeyer then immediately turned left and got off a burst at the other Fw 190, which took fire and went straight in twisting and smoking. You can imagine my frustration in not getting one of those for myself, but the fact is that Harmeyer did exactly what a sharp fighter pilot should do. They were right in front of him, I was lagging behind, so he shot them both down within about ten seconds. I was in a few air battles that winter, but never a turkey shoot like that one.'

Elsewhere that day, 2Lt 'Junior' Adams of the 2nd FS claimed his only Spitfire victory, but he was to score four further kills, one of them shared, as well as two unconfirmed victories on Mustangs by early June. On Corsica, the 4th FS sent a detachment to Ghisonaccia, on the southeast coast, to perform escort work with the B-25 squadron based there.

One of 'Dixie' Alexander's last Spitfire VCs is seen here after its withdrawal from service. This machine is believed to be the aircraft in which he made his final Spitfire claims in February 1944. Behind it is an aircraft from the 309th FS (*via Wojtek Matusiak*)

Maj Garth Jared assumed command of the 309th FS on 9 November 1943, and retained this position until the following April, during which time he claimed two Spitfire victories (*31st FW Aviano*)

1Lt Leland Molland (left), who claimed 4.5 of his 10.5 victories in the Spitfire, relaxes with his 308th FS CO, Maj James Thorsen, who was credited with two kills, including one in the British fighter (*H Levy via Norman Franks*)

The bitter fighting on the 'Gustav Line', which had the great monastery at Monte Cassino at its heart, also continued unabated. On 16 February the monastery was bombed, while the 309th continued to patrol the Anzio beachhead, encountering more enemy fighters. In the subsequent battle, unit CO Maj Garth Jared latched onto an Fw 190, and his fire caused pieces to fly off the German fighter before it crashed in flames next to a road near Valmontone.

One of the leading, albeit least known, MTO aces was 1Lt Robert C Curtis (later CO of the 2nd FS), who claimed 14 victories – 13 of them in the Mustang. His first came when flying a Spitfire VB on 19 February during a sweep over the Viterbo area. Two dozen Spitfires were challenged by a large number of Fw 190s and Bf 109s, and in the huge dogfight that ensued, there were losses on both sides. Curtis reported;

'Other Spits attacked, and one German fighter levelled out in front of me about a thousand yards away. I closed to about 200 yards, directly behind and slightly below it, and fired about a one-second burst of cannon and machine gun fire, but observed no strikes. I had no gun sight because the light bulb had burned out. We were both at about 6000 ft, and as I fired the burst, the enemy aircraft flicked over and headed straight down. I rolled over and followed it. As it started a medium turn to the left, I fired another two-second burst from about 200 yards behind and slightly above it. I saw strikes all over the fuselage and wings of the enemy aircraft. About 500 ft off the ground it flipped onto its back, flew on into the ground on the side of a hill and broke up about five miles west of San Lorenzo Nuovo.'

Curtis' victim is believed to have been Oblt Rolf Klippingen of 7./JG 53.

Also successful during this mission was his friend, and tent mate, 1Lt 'Dixie' Alexander, who also claimed his own third victory. Having remained above as top cover, he spotted three unengaged Bf 109Gs, as he later recalled;

'Two of the enemy aircraft peeled off in a southeasterly direction, and one did a port turn and headed northeast. Apparently, I had not been observed. After making sure that the first two aircraft were indeed leaving the scene, I went to full boost in my Spit IX and went after the Me 109. It was letting down, and still going northeast. This in itself was an advantage, because it took me towards the coast, and home. I continued to follow him as he let down at 300 mph, not losing or gaining any ground.

'The enemy aircraft elected to fly up a valley between two mountain ridges. I closed to about 300 yards and gave him a short burst of both machine gun and cannon. I immediately had a pull to the right on my aircraft, and knew that my starboard cannon was not firing. I saw no strikes, and continued to close to about 150 yards, firing another short burst. Again I saw no strikes. I closed to 100 yards and gave him a long burst of both cannon and machine gun, while holding hard on rudder and control column to keep the aircraft from swinging. This time I had good solid bursts in the fuselage and right behind the cockpit. The enemy aircraft immediately nosed violently down and crashed directly into the ground. There was an explosion, but when I pulled up to do a 180-degree turn and fly over the wreck, there was no sign of fire.

The 308th FS's 1Lt Molland hailed from North Dakota, and christened his allocated Spitfire VIII *FARGO express* after the stagecoach company of the same name. It is seen here after being marked with his fifth victory, which he achieved on 22 February 1944. The white swastika is for a probable claimed two days earlier (*W Skinner via C F Shores*)

'I can't imagine how I was able to fire three successive bursts without the pilot of the 109 knowing that he was being attacked. Although the mountain pass was narrow, he still had room to manoeuvre. I can only assume that he was thinking of home, sausage and good German beer. So much for air combat!'

Over Anzio, the 309th had also been busy in the morning, with an early beachhead patrol attacking 20+ intruders at about 21,000 ft. Amongst those who engaged the enemy was 1Lt Mick Ainley, who caught a Bf 109 heading for Rome and closed to 300 yards, before hitting it with two short bursts that struck the fighter's radiator and caused the latter to stream glycol and then thick smoke. However, as he overshot he lost sight of the enemy, and so his final Spitfire claim was only a damaged – he reached 'acedom' during April when flying P-51s. Later that same day 2Lt Robert Belmont destroyed a Bf 109 that crashed near the mouth of the River Tiber.

Then, after several days of intense enemy action, the 309th FS flew ground attack missions near Anzio on 20 February, and these were opposed by a handful of enemy fighters. In the resulting dogfight, future six-kill Spitfire VIII ace 1Lt Richard Hurd shot down a Bf 109G and damaged another, while fellow future ace 1Lt Leland 'Tommy' Molland claimed an Fw 190 as a probable after it was last seen limping out of the battle at very low altitude.

The following day, as the weather steadily improved, 1Lt Fred Trafton of the 308th FS, who later achieved five victories in Mustangs, hit and damaged a Bf 109 for his first ever claim. The 308th's total increased further on the 22nd, when, just before 0900 hrs, a patrol over Anzio had a hot engagement with around 30 enemy aircraft. In the resulting action 'Tommy' Molland used his Spitfire to shoot down two Bf 109Gs, thus taking his growing tally to 4.5 kills. Another Messerschmitt fell to Richard Hurd for his third victory, while others were claimed by squadron CO Maj James Thorsen, as well as

One of a number of USAAF aces that cut their teeth flying the Spitfire, although he did not claim any victories with the aircraft, 2Lt Dan Zoerb of the 2nd FS was described as having 'all the flying abilities you could ask for. He was a good tactician, and missed nothing. He had excellent eyes, coordination and the ability to act on a moment's notice in any situation' (*via Norman Franks*)

Another USAAF ace who made his early claims with the Spitfire was 1Lt Ray Harmeyer of the 309th FS, who shot down two Fw 190s over Anzio on 13 February 1944 to begin his path to 'acedom'. He baled out in early March and was rescued by an RAF Walrus (*R Harmeyer via Norman Franks*)

Lts Walker and Brown (this was the latter pilot's third victory). Elsewhere, however, 1Lt Hackbarth was shot down in flames.

The 31st FG remained incredibly active in the skies over Anzio through to late February 1944, in spite of the near incessant rain, with operations continuing unabated whenever the weather was suitable. One of the occasional claims during this period was made by 1Lt Dick Faxon of the 309th, who, on the 29th, managed to get behind a lone Fw 190 and open fire from 100 yards. He described afterwards how 'it seemed to open up like a can of chilli' as strikes lit up the enemy fighter from nose to tail and it disintegrated in the air just as the pilot baled out. This was his only Spitfire victory, but he claimed four more flying the P-51B during bomber escort missions over Rumania during the spring 1944 air offensive.

THE LAST HURRAHS!

In his official report on the 31st FG's activities for the month of March, Maj Albert Levy recorded, 'The group was operating from Castel Volturno landing ground, a pierced steel planking strip near the mouth of the Volturno River. The weather was mild. Col Charles M McCorkle continued to command, leading the group on some missions, and directing operations'.

The 52nd FG too continued on fighter-bomber and escort operations, and at the end of February it had come under the command of Lt Col Robert Levine, who had three victories to his name.

During the mid morning of 3 March, the 2nd FS provided escort for 48 B-26 Marauders, but as they approached the Italian coast, 2Lt 'Junior' Adams suffered an engine failure and baled out, as he later described;

'As I was gliding down, with "Blue 4" following, I tried to drop the belly tank but it would not release. At 7000 ft I released my harness, rolled the trim wheel forward and tried to roll the Spitfire over so that I would fall out, but it would not roll because of its slow speed, and because I still had on the nearly full 90-gallon belly drop tank. At about 4000 ft, I gave the stick a hard push forward and was thrown clear of the aircraft. I was going down vertically when I pulled the rip cord, and the parachute opened immediately.'

Adams had been covered by future seven-victory ace 2Lt Dan Zoerb, who stayed above him until the rescue Walrus arrived. Adams was not the only USAAF Spitfire pilot to be grateful for the presence of the antiquated-looking RAF amphibian.

The focus for 31st FG squadrons continued to be Anzio, and soon after taking off for a patrol on 7 March Ray Harmeyer baled out after an engine failure. Upon entering the water he got tangled in his rigging, but he too was successfully rescued by a Walrus.

As the weather at last began to improve so more flying was possible, including some sweeps over southern France by the 52nd FG. The end for the USAAF Spitfires began, however, on 11 March when Col McCorkle brought in the first of the replacement P-51Bs for the 31st FG and promptly gave a demonstration to his sceptical pilots in a mock fight with a Spitfire. Nevertheless, someone noted that the British fighter 'completely outmanoeuvred the new Mustang'!

It was still very much business as usual for the group though, as 48 hours later, during a beachhead patrol at about 1715 hrs, two intruders were reported. An Fw 190 and a Bf 109G were spotted as they dived away, but 1Lts Elmer Livingstone and Maurice Vaughn of the 307th were in the immediate vicinity and destroyed them both.

Yet another future ace had reason to be thankful to the RAF rescue service during one of the last operations with the Spitfire when the 2nd FS flew a ground attack mission along the Italian coast on 18 March. Leading Red Section was 1Lt Bob Curtis, who recalled;

'I went down to strafe a barrack-like building while the rest of the flight orbited. I fired from 1000 ft, and had started to break away at an altitude of 500 ft when my aircraft was hit by a terrific explosion when the building unexpectedly blew up. The engine of my Spitfire immediately quit, and I lost control of the machine until it emerged from the smoke and fire. At 1500 ft, with the IAS at 100 mph, it was now time for me to cut the throttle. Disconnecting everything, I stepped onto the seat, put one foot on the door hinges and shoved off. I saw the tail of the Spitfire pass and then pulled the ripcord. I entered the water about five miles southwest of Cecina Marina. I settled down and waited for the RAF Walrus.'

While the 52nd FG continued to fly fighter-bomber missions, the 31st FG remained active over Anzio and Cassino. On the 18th, the group flew more than 100 sorties and engaged about 80 enemy fighters around Cassino. During the fighting, the 308th FS downed two aircraft, one of which fell to 1Lt Richard Hurd, while the 307th also destroyed two enemy fighters. Later that same day, the 307th downed two more Fw 190s, one of which fell to Lt Carroll Pryblo for his third victory. Then, near Pignataro, in the early afternoon of 21 March, 1Lt Richard Hurd, in a Spitfire VIII, shot down a pair of Bf 109s (that he identified as elderly 'Emils') to become the USAAF's final Spitfire ace. Maj Levy, in the 31st FG's official record, noted this significant event thus;

The last USAAF pilot to become an ace with the Spitfire was 1Lt Richard Hurd of the 308th FS, who achieved this distinction on 21 March, shortly before the type's withdrawal (*W Skinner via C F Shores*)

Another pilot who had reason to be grateful to the RAF's antiquated Walrus was 2nd FS CO Maj Bert Sanborn, who, on 11 April, just before his unit's Spitfires were replaced with Mustangs, was hit by flak and he was forced to bale out into the sea. Amongst those who flew top cover for him were future aces 'Dixie' Alexander and 2Lt 'Sully' Varnell (*B Sandborn via Norman Franks*)

When shot down, Sanborn was described as 'flying his uniquely light-coloured aircraft', which may have been this unusually camouflaged Spitfire IX of the 52nd FG, seen in early 1944 plugged into its trolley-acc at a Corsican airfield prior to flying yet another sortie (*via Wojtek Matusiak*)

'The 308th FS finally managed to top the 309th FS's score in enemy aircraft destroyed – 309th has 60, and today the 308th destroyed four ME 109s to bring its score to 61. Lt Hurd bagged two of them, bringing his personal score to six destroyed (making him an ace), one probably destroyed and two damaged.'

The following day, Fred Trafton was leading a formation of six Spitfire VIIIs over Cassino when they ran into 50+ Fw 190s and Bf 109s, two of which fell to Lt Roche to take his total to three. Trafton also damaged one, which was the future ace's last claim with the British fighter.

Despite the groups' imminent re-equipment, new pilots arriving in-theatre began their operational training on Spitfires – and most wanted the chance to fly the British legend. One was 2Lt Bob Goebel who, through the summer of 1944, would achieve 11 victories. Before finally converting to the Mustang, Charles McCorkle was given permission for a final fling, and on 29 March he led a 36-aircraft sweep over Rome, during which some Fw 190s were intercepted and 1Lt Leonard Emery of the 308th destroyed one. The first of his four victories was also the last by a Spitfire of the 31st FG, which flew its first Mustang mission in the middle of April.

The 52nd FG remained operational on Spitfires into April 1944, however, and on the 6th, the 2nd and 5th FSs escorted a B-26 raid against the railway bridge at Ficulle. The top cover of Spitfire IXs from the 5th FS was bounced by six Bf 109s, and in the resulting action 2Lt Joe Blackburn shot down two of them to claim the last USAAF Spitfire victories.

Fighter-bombing operations continued, and losses still happened, beyond this date, as on the 11th when 2nd FS CO Maj Bert Sanborn led a sweep from Borgo north along the Italian coast. They dive-bombed a railway yard at Leghorn, but Sanborn was hit by deadly light flak and baled out eight miles off the coast. His squadron flew top cover for him, with future aces 1Lts 'Dixie' Alexander and 'Sully' Varnell being the last to leave when fuel ran short. Their CO was rescued soon after by an Air-Sea Rescue Walrus from the RAF's No 284 Sqn detachment that was also based at Bastia.

Three days later, the first of the 52nd FG's Mustangs arrived, with the 2nd and 5th FSs beginning their conversion immediately. The 4th FS commenced changing fighter types on the 20th in preparation for the new long-range escort role that the group would now be tasked with flying. 'Dixie' Alexander flew his last mission in a Spitfire on 15 May, when he dive-bombed a bridge at Grosetto and then strafed trucks at Poggibonsi. He recalled his mount with affection, his words probably echoing the opinion of most of his colleagues. 'My experience in Spitfires was thoroughly satisfying. They were just so much a part of you when you flew, and they were tough, durable, reliable little aeroplanes with plenty of punch'.

Of the leading USAAF aces in the Mediterranean, several of the top-scoring pilots had cut their teeth on the Spitfire, although some did not make any claims on them. Both the USAAF fighter groups had flown their British fighters with great distinction in almost two years of operations. The 31st FG was credited with a total of 192 enemy aircraft destroyed, and no less than ten aces had been created flying the Spitfire – a further eight claimed at least some of their totals with the British fighter. Having latterly concentrated on fighter-bomber work, the 52nd FG was slightly behind the 31st with 164 victories. Three Spitfire aces had been produced, with a further five aces making some claims in the aircraft.

The American pilots had certainly got the most out of their 'reverse lend lease' fighters!

THE LAST VICTORIES

Although the last USAAF Spitfire fighter squadron in Italy had begun re-equipment in late April 1944, a month later, Spitfire Vs were being issued to a new American squadron in England! It was not, however, a USAAF unit, but instead the only US Navy squadron to fly the British fighter. To spot for the fire of US and British warships during the planned invasion of France, a number of units were trained for this crucial role, and as the US Navy's spotting unit in the UK flew vulnerable floatplanes, it was re-equipped with fighters.

Thus, in early May, catapult flights from several US Navy battleships and cruisers formed as VCS-7 at RNAS Lee-on-Solent, in Hampshire, which was to be the unit's operational base. VCS-7's pilots underwent type conversion with the USAAF's PR Spitfire-equipped 67th Reconnaissance Group at Membury, after which Lt Cdr William Denton took command of the unit. His squadron began taking delivery of its own Spitfire VBs, which wore British markings, on the 29th.

VCS-7's first sorties commenced early on D-Day, 6 June, with the unit providing pairs of Spitfires to their allocated warships, as the latter pounded the enemy defences on the beaches. As predicted, the spotting sorties did prove vulnerable, and US Navy pilots were engaged by both fighters and accurate light flak – the unit lost one aircraft during the 39 sorties flown that day. VCS-7 pilots occasionally encountered the Luftwaffe, and although official records remain unclear as to whether they engaged enemy aircraft in combat, a Spitfire did carry a kill marking. What is known is that Ens Carmichael and his wingman were intercepted by a Bf 109 on one mission, although they evaded successfully.

By 15 June there were far fewer missions to be flown, as in VCS-7's sector in the west the American advance had put targets outside the range of the ships' guns. On the 26th the unit stood down, having gained a small niche in the annals of US naval aviation history.

While US Navy pilots were spotting for the guns, other Americans were also flying Spitfire VBs over the beaches. One was Flt Lt David Fairbanks from New York, who, during No 501 Sqn's first patrol over the beachhead at dawn on 8 June, gained his unit's first kill since the invasion. The squadron history described how the patrol went;

'Vectored to the scene of Luftwaffe activity. Changing course, more enemy aircraft were reported on the squadron's flank, so Yellow Section detached itself and spotted six Me 109s below them, heading away from Le Havre. Flt Lt

VCS-7 was the only US Navy squadron to fly the Spitfire, which it used for bombardment spotting during the D-Day landings. Lt Robert Doyle and Ens John Mudge congratulate each other after helping break up an enemy armoured column on 10 June 1944 (*US Navy*)

Flt Lt David 'Foob' Fairbanks of No 501 Sqn claimed his only Spitfire victory on 8 June when he shot down a Bf 109 near Le Havre and damaged another. He extended his total to 12.5 victories after converting to the Tempest (*C H Thomas*)

"Foob" Fairbanks, the piano-playing American, tore into the enemy fighters, sending one down in flames and badly damaging another.'

These successes over Deauville were Fairbanks' only ones in the Spitfire, although he was to gain a further 11.5 kills in Tempests.

One month later, on 5 July, Flg Off 'Tex' Davenport, who earlier in the year had been shot down and evaded capture to rejoin No 401 Sqn just in time for D-Day, opened his account. Patrolling northwest of Chartres in a Spitfire IXB at around midday, Davenport achieved his first victory when he shot down an Fw 190. Twelve days later, while patrolling near Cabourg at dusk, he shot down a Do 217.

Another American pilot with the RCAF to enjoy success during this period was Flt Lt Henry Zary of No 421 Sqn, who had gained his first kill on 28 June when he downed a Bf 109 near Caen. Then, on 25 July, he achieved a notable feat during a sweep, as he later recalled;

'I was flying east, leading "B" Flight in the Les Andelys area at 10,000 ft, when 40+ Me 109s were sighted at 10,000-15,000 ft on a reciprocal course. I broke to the right as the enemy aircraft opened fire. After an orbit to starboard, I followed two who pulled up climbing, one of them turning to port and diving. I fired at the latter and saw strikes on its starboard wing tip, then the enemy aircraft straightened out and dived gently. The pilot then jettisoned his coupe top and baled out. The 'chute did not open.'

Having despatched a second Messerschmitt fighter, Zary climbed to rejoin his section, whereupon more Bf 109s were spotted;

'I fired at the last enemy aircraft, who dived to the deck, and I followed. I was out of ammunition, but remained above and behind him, reporting the enemy's position, and my lack of ammunition, to my squadron leader. I then dived on the enemy anyhow. The aircraft turned sharply to starboard to evade, apparently hit a tree, then stalled into the ground.'

Largely as a result of this engagement, Zary was awarded the DFC.

The RCAF Spitfire squadrons, with their handful of Americans, supported the breakout from Normandy and the headlong rush north towards Holland, where, in mid-September, they became embroiled in the desperate fighting around Arnhem. Having been credited with four confirmed victories since returning to the squadron, 'Tex' Davenport had certainly made his mark. And by early October he was based with No 401 Sqn at the airstrip at B 84 Rips, in Holland. It was from here, on 5 October, that Davenport was to participate in a significant action, as the unit's war diary recounted;

'Twelve aircraft took off, and while on patrol, an ME 262 was spotted diving towards Nijmegen. The squadron promptly dived after it, and following a chase, during which five members of the squadron took a squirt at it, the enemy aircraft started to burn in the air and finally crashed on friendly territory. This ME 262 shot down today is the first one destroyed by either the RCAF or RAF.'

Having avoided a near collision with his CO's Spitfire, Davenport had eventually opened fire on the Me 262, as he later recalled;

'I finally closed in to 300 yards line astern and emptied the remainder of my guns – approximately 10 or 12 seconds – into the kite, observing strikes in the engines and fuselage. The aircraft was burning all this time. The pilot seemed to be unhurt, and put up a good fight during all this.'

Their victim was Me 262 9K+BL of I./KG(J) 51, flown by Hptm Christoph Burtmann, who was killed when he baled out too low. 'Tex' Davenport's significant final claim also took him to 'acedom' with four and one shared victories.

THE LAST ACE

Even at this late stage of the war, there was still a handful of Americans joining RCAF units. One was Flt Lt Don Pieri, a Texan who had served in Canada as a flying instructor prior to joining Spitfire IXE-equipped No 442 Sqn in November 1944. Shortly after his assignment to the unit, it moved to Volkel, in Holland. Poor weather interfered with operations for much of December, but at lunchtime on the last day of the year he took part in an armed reconnaissance. South of Munster around midday, the Canadian Spitfires ran into some Bf 109s and shot down four of them, one of which was chased and harried by Flt Lts Perkins and Pieri until it crashed into a small hill. The share was the American's first success.

1944 had ended well for No 442 Sqn, and the New Year also began in spectacular fashion. The squadron was airborne when the Luftwaffe launched its massive attack on Allied air bases at dawn, and just west of Venlo its pilots encountered around 40 enemy fighters. The squadron shot down a number of them, with two Focke-Wulfs falling to Pieri, who also damaged two more. On 18 March he joined No 412 Sqn at B 88 Heesch, and as dusk fell on the 25th, he shot down a Bf 109 to the west of Winterswijk.

The unit moved into Germany soon afterwards and established itself at B 108 Rheine, from where a No 412 Sqn section encountered some of the few remaining airworthy Luftwaffe fighters during an early patrol over Hagenow on 19 April. Don Pieri, flying Spitfire IXE NH471, destroyed an Fw 190 and shared in the destruction of a second with Flt Lt L A Stewart, thus becoming an ace.

Even at this late stage of the war, Pieri was not, however, to be the last American to become a Spitfire ace. On 16 February, Henry Zary had been promoted to command No 403 Sqn at Evere, near Brussels, flying Spitfire XVIs in support of the advance of the Anglo-Canadian 21st Army

Texan Flt Lt Don Pieri claimed his first three victories flying Spitfire IXs with No 442 Sqn either side of New Year's Day 1945. He was based at B 88 Heesch, where Y2-B sits at readiness on a steel matting dispersal (*A J Mallandaine*)

Group into North-West Germany. By mid April No 403 Sqn was based just inside Germany at Goch, from where in the late afternoon of 21 April, Zary, flying Spitfire XVI TB752/KH-Z, downed a Bf 109 near Schnackenburg to become the final American Spitfire ace of World War 2. He subsequently reported;

'I was "Kapok" leader on an Armed Recce in the Parchim area, when returning, I sighted two Me 109s apparently attacking ground targets. They were climbing when we gave chase. They climbed to about 7000 ft, and I closed on the starboard aircraft, telling Flg Off Leslie to take the port one. Closing to 600 yards, line astern, I opened fire with a four-second burst to 400 yards, strikes cutting a third of the starboard wing, fin and rudder off. Strikes were also observed on the cockpit, and the aircraft crashed out of control.'

The Spitfire XVI Zary was flying had only been delivered to the squadron two days earlier, and on the 25th, whilst being flown by Flg Off Leslie, it destroyed another enemy aircraft, thought to be an Fw 189. Then, on 1 May, when flown by Flg Off Young, the fighter claimed its third kill – an Fw 190. During a strafe of Schwenrin airfield four days after becoming an ace, Zary damaged an Me 262 and a Ju 88 on the ground to make his final claims.

The last American ace to claim a kill when flying a Spitfire was, however, Flt Lt Don Pieri. It was made during an armed reconnaissance on the evening of 30 April, as he described in his combat report;

'About 15 miles east of Hamburg I saw four FW 190s heading east on the deck as I was heading north. They turned and flew northwest, while I gave chase. When I got in range, two broke to starboard on the deck and two to port up into cloud. I got a good shot of three seconds from about 20-30 degrees at one on the deck at 400 yards. I had to break off combat and break to port into the two FW 190s, which had gone into cloud. They both overshot me and I got a squirt at one. Just before I opened fire on the second 190, I saw one of the other two explode as it hit the deck. I took a quick squirt at the second 190 and then broke up into cloud.'

However, in a tragic twist of fate, on 3 May, while carrying out a strafing attack near Keil, Pieri's Spitfire was hit by his own ricochets and he was forced to bale out. Listed as missing, his body was never found, and he was possibly a victim of the savage summary justice sometimes meted out to Allied airmen by the enemy in the final weeks of the war.

The last American to become a Spitfire ace was Sqn Ldr Henry 'Hank' Zary from New York, who was the CO of No 403 Sqn RCAF. His fifth victory came when he shot down a Bf 109 on 21 April. Sadly, he succumbed to pleurisy soon after the war (*C H Thomas*)

Sqn Ldr 'Hank' Zary was flying this Spitfire XVI (TB752) when he claimed his fifth victory on 21 April 1945. The aircraft survived the war and is now on display at the Spitfire Memorial Museum at Manston, in Kent (*C H Thomas*)

APPENDICES

American Spitfire Aces

Name	Unit/s	Spitfire Claims	Total Claims	Theatre/s
Lynch J J	71, 249	10+7sh/1/1.5	10+7sh/1/1.5	UK, MedME
Weaver C	412, 185, 403	12.5/3/-	12.5/3/-	MedME, UK
Wade L C	145	10/1/7	22+2sh/1/7	MedME
Feld S	4th FS	9/-/1	9/-/1	MedME
Gladych B M	303, 302	8/2/0.5	18/2/0.5	UK
McColpin C W	71, 121, 133, 336th FS	8/0/2	8/0/3+3 unconf dest	UK
McDonald N L	2nd FS	7.5/2/4	11.5/2/4	UK, MedME
Curry J H	601, 80	7+1sh/2/4	7+1sh/2/4	UK, MedME
Hill F A	308th FS, 309th FS, 31st FG	6+2sh/2/5	6+2sh/2/5	UK, MedME
Jones R O	611, 126	6+2sh/1/3	6+2sh/1/3	UK, MedME
Tilley R F	121, 601, 126	7/2/5	7/2/5	UK, MedME
Peterson C G	71, 4th FG	6/2/3	7/4/7	UK
Collinsworth J D	307th FS	6/1+1sh/1	6/1+1sh/1	UK, MedME
Hurd R F	308th FS	6/1/2	6/1/2	MedME
Fields V C Jr	307th FS	6/-/2	6/-/2	MedME
Pieri D M	442, 412	6/-/2	6/-/2	Eur
Vinson A E	2nd FS, 5th FS	5+1sh/-/1.5	5+1sh/-/1.5	UK, MedMe
Gimbel E L	401, 403, 421	4+2sh/1.5/1	4+2sh/1.5/1	UK
Cabas V N	403, 4th FS	4+2sh/-/-	4+2sh/-/-	UK, MedME
White J H	307th FS	5/2sh/1	5/2sh/1	UK, MedME
Edner S R	121, 336th FS, 4th FG	5/0.5/2	5/0.5/2	UK
Fischette C R	307th FS	5/0.5/1	5/0.5/1	MedME
Payne C W	309th FS	5/2/3	5/2/3	UK, MedME
Thyng H R	309th FS	5/2/3	10/3/7	UK, MedME
Johnson P G	421	5/-/3	5/-/3	UK
Mahon J B	121	5/1/2	5/1/2	UK
Zary H P M	421, 403	5/-/2	5/-/2	UK, Eur
McCorkle C M	31st FG	5/-/-	11/-/1	MedME
Peck J E	121, 126, 2nd FS	4.5/4/8+3sh	4.5/4/8+3sh	UK, MedME
Molland L P	308th FS	4.5/1/-	10.5/1/-	MedME
Carey J A	5th FS	4.5/-/2	4.5/-/2	MedME
Davenport R M	401	4+1sh/-/1	4+1sh/-/1	UK, Eur
Fletcher M K	403, 4th FS	4.5/-/-	4.5/-/-	UK, MedME
Butler J E	2nd FS	4.5/-/-	4.5/-/-	MedME
Coen O H	71, 334th FS, 336th FS	2+3sh/0.5/2	2+4sh/0.5/3	UK
Daley W J*	121, 335th FS	2.5/-/3	2.5/-/3	UK
Donahue A G *	71, 91	2/1/2	2/1/2	UK

Notes

Multiple shared claims are shown thus '+3sh', which indicates three half/part shares, in addition to any full claims. Those pilots with less than five victories are marked thus *, and are shown because of their inclusion in Christopher Shores' *Aces High* or Frank Olynyk's *Stars & Bars*, or where there may be doubt as to their actual scores

Theatre Abbreviations

UK - United Kingdom
MedME - Malta, Mediterranean, North Africa and Italy
Eur - France and Germany post D-Day

American Aces with some Spitfire Claims

Name	Unit/s	Spitfire Claims	Total Claims	Theatre/s
Adams J A	2nd FS	1/-/-	4.5/-/-	MedME
Ainley J M	309th FS	2/1/1	7+2sh/3/3	MedMe
Aitken J Jr	2nd FS	1.5/-/-	4.5/-/2	MedME
Alexander R L	133, 336th FS, 109th OS, 2nd FS	3/1/-	5/1/-	UK, MedME
Baker R N	308th FS	3/1/2	15+3sh/2/3	MedME
Blakeslee D J M	401, 133, 336th FS	3/3/7	14.5/3/11	UK
Burnett R L III	4th FS	2/0.5/-	5/0.5/1	MedME
Clark J A Jr	71, 334th FS	0.5/-/-	10.5/-/2	UK
Cleaveland A B	601	-/-/1	5/-/1	MedME
Curtis R C	2nd FS	1/-/-	14/1/5	MedME
Daymond G A	71, 334th FS	4/0/1	7/0/1	UK
Dillard W J	307th FS	-/-/1	6/3/3	MedME
Dunn W R	71, 130	2/-/-	6/0.5/-	UK
Evans R W	121, 335th FS	1/-/-	6/-/2	UK
Fairbanks D C	501	1/-/1	12.5/-/3	UK, Eur
Faxon R D	309th FS	1/-/1	5/-/4	MedME
Gentile D S	133, 336th FS	2/-/1	21+2sh/-/3	UK
Harmeyer R F	309th FS	2/-/1	6/1/4	MedME
Jacobs J A	308th FS	1/-/-	4.5/1/1	MedME
Johnson A G	2nd FS	2/-/1	8.5/-/1	MedME
McLaughlin M D	309th FS	-/-/1	7/1/6	MedME
McPharlin M G H	71, 334th FS	3sh/0.5/1	1+4sh/0.5/4	UK
Ohr F	2nd FS	1/-/-	6/-/-	MedME
Powers M	145	2+1sh/-/1.5	7+1sh/-/1.5	MedME
Shafer D E Jr	309th FS	4/-/1	7/-/3	UK, MedME
Thorne J N	402, 64, 504	1+2sh/1sh/1	4+2sh/1sh/4	UK
Trafton F O Jr	308th FS	-/-/2	5/1/3	MedME
Tyler J O	4th FS	2/-/-	8/-/1	MedME
Vineyard M W	185	-/-/1	6/-/1	MedME
Wynn V H	603, 249	1+1sh/2/2	3+2sh/2/3	MedME

USAAF Aces who flew Spitfires but made no Claims

Name	Spitfire Unit/s	Total Claims	Theatre
Beeson D W	71, 334th FS	17+1sh/1/3	UK
Brooks J L	307th FS	13/1/2	MedME
Brown S J	309th FS	15.5/1/7	MedME
Care R C	71, 334th FS	6/1/0	UK
Carpenter G	121, 335th FS	13+2sh/1/8	UK
Chick L W	336th FS	6/-/-	UK
France V J	334th FS	4+1sh /-/-	UK
Gabreski F S	315	34.5/1/5	UK
Goebel R J	308th FS	11/1/0	MedME
Goodson J A	416, 133, 336th FS	14/1/1	UK
Hively H D	71, 334th FS	12/1/1	UK
Lawler J B	2nd FS	11/2/3	MedME
Loving G G Jr	309th FS	5/-/2	MedME
McKennon P W	335th FS	10+2sh/-/2.5	UK
Mills H J	71, 334th FS	6/2/1	UK
Pisanos S N	71, 334th FS	5/0/1	UK
Smith K G	121, 335th FS	4+2sh/-/1	UK
Varnell J S	2nd FS	17/0/2	MedME
Wilhelm D C	309th FS	6/1/3	MedME
Zoerb D J	2nd FS	7/-/-	MedME

USAAF Spitfire Groups

4th Fighter Group

CO - Col E W Anderson

334th Fighter Squadron
Unit Code - XR
When Spitfire-equipped - September 1942 to March 1943
Mark/s - V
Theatre/s - UK
COs - Maj G A Daymond

335th Fighter Squadron
Unit Code - AV
When Spitfire-equipped - September 1942 to March 1943
Mark/s -V
Theatre/s - UK
COs - Maj W J Daley and Maj D J M Blakeslee

336th Fighter Squadron
Unit Code - MD
When Spitfire-equipped - September 1942 to March 1943
Mark/s - V
Theatre/s - UK
COs - Maj C W McColpin and Maj O H Coen

31st Fighter Group

COs - Col J R Hawkins, Lt Col F M Dean, Lt Col F A Hill and
Lt Col C M McCorkle

307th Fighter Squadron
Unit Code - MX
When Spitfire-equipped - July 1942 to March 1944
Mark/s - V, VIII and IX
Theatre/s - UK, MedME
COs - Capt G J La Breche, Capt M P Davis, Capt V C Fields
and Maj A C Gillem

308th Fighter Squadron
Unit Code - HL
When Spitfire-equipped - July 1942 to March 1944
Mark/s - V, VIII and IX
Theatre/s - UK, MedME
COs - Maj F M Dean, Maj D B Avery, Capt T D Fleming,
Capt J H Paulk, Maj W J Overend and Maj J G Thorsen

309th Fighter Squadron
Unit Code - WZ
When Spitfire-equipped - July 1942 to March 1944
Mark/s - V, VIII and IX
Theatre/s - UK, MedME
COs - Maj H R Thyng, Maj F A Hill, Maj C W Payne and
Capt G B Jared

52nd Fighter Group

COs - Col D M Allison, Lt Col G W West, Lt Col J S Coward,
Lt Col R A Ames, Col M L McNickle and Lt Col R Levine

2nd Fighter Squadron
Unit Code - QP
When Spitfire-equipped - July 1942 to April 1944
Mark/s - V, VIII and IX
Theatre/s - UK, MedME
COs - Lt R E Keyes, Capt J S Coward, Maj G V Williams
and Capt B S Sanborn

4th Fighter Squadron
Unit Code - WD
When Spitfire-equipped - July 1942 to April 1944
Mark/s - V, VIII and IX
Theatre/s - UK, MedME
COs - Maj R Levine, Maj Houston and Capt Trowbridge

5th Fighter Squadron
Unit Code - VF
When Spitfire-equipped - July 1942 to April 1944
Mark/s - V, VIII and IX
Theatre/s - UK, MedME
COs - Capt G C Deaton and Capt E K Jenkins

496th Fighter Training Group

555th Fighter Training Squadron
Unit Code - C7
When Spitfire-equipped - December 1943 to early 1944
Mark/s - V and IX
Theatre/s - UK

Colour Plates

1

Spitfire IIA P7308/XR-D of Plt Off W R Dunn, No 71 'Eagle' Sqn, North Weald, 27 August 1941

Initially flying Hurricane IIs with No 71 Sqn, Plt Off Bill Dunn had claimed three Bf 109s destroyed with the Hawker fighter during July and August 1941. Squadronmate Plt Off 'Gus' Daymond had also claimed three kills in the Hurricane, and there was much interest in which of them would be the first to reach the magic 'five'. During mid-August No 71 Sqn was re-equipped with Spitfre IIs, and on the 27th the unit formed part of an escort for a bombing raid on the steelworks in Lille. Passing over the French coast just north of Boulogne, No 71 Sqn's Spitfires, including Dunn in this aircraft, were attacked by Bf 109s, and in the resulting fight he shot two German fighters down. He thus became the first American ace of World War 2. However, as his second victim fell away, fire from another Bf 109 hit his aircraft and, badly injured, Dunn limped back across the Channel to land safely at Hawkinge, on the Kent coast. P7308 was repaired and saw further lengthy service.

2

Spitfire VB AB908/XR-Y of Plt Off C W McColpin, No 71 'Eagle' Sqn, North Weald, September-October 1941

In September 1941 No 71 Sqn received cannon-armed Spitfire VBs, and with these it continued to conduct offensive operations into northern France. One of its pilots during this period was 'Red' McColpin (who had previously served with Nos 67 and 121 Sqns), and he was flying this aircraft along the French coast to the west of Lille on the afternoon of 21 September when he downed a Bf 109E for his first victory. McColpin was at the controls of AB908 once again on 2 October as part of a bomber escort when his unit was attacked near Abbeville by Bf 109s. He sighted one, and firing a short burst, set it on fire and the pilot baled out. Having helped scatter the enemy, McColpin dived on another German fighter and opened fire, following it down until it hit the ground. By the end of the month he had claimed three more victories to become the first American ace to score at least five kills with the Spitfire. AB908 later served with No 121 'Eagle' Sqn, before being converted into a Seafire.

3

Spitfire VB BL287/XR-C of Plt Off L Nomis, No 71 'Eagle' Sqn, Martlesham Heath, 17 April 1942

Although not an ace, Leo Nomis had a long and varied combat career, and made his initial claim for a 'damaged' in January 1942. His first confirmed success came when flying this aircraft on 17 April, which he shared with future Spitfire ace Plt Off John Lynch, who also registered his first success on this date in Spitfire VB W3740. During an early morning patrol off the coast at Felixstowe, they both spotted a Ju 88 at wave top height and fired on it, although Lynch's aircraft was hit and he was forced home with his fighter damaged. Leo Nomis continued to make quarter attacks on the bomber, which eventually emitted black smoke and plunged into the sea. Of mixed Irish and Sioux Indian parentage, Nomis decorated his Spitfire with an Indian Chief's head. He later

served in Malta and Egypt, transferred to the USAAF and after World War 2 saw more action with the embryonic Israeli Air Force, where he flew Czech-built S 199s (Junkers Jumo-engined Bf 109Gs)!

4

Spitfire VB BL753/YO-H of Plt Off D J W Blakeslee, No 401 Sqn RCAF, Gravesend, April-May 1942

One of the greatest American fighter leaders of World War 2, Don Blakeslee initially served with the RCAF's No 401 Sqn, with which he claimed one destroyed, two probables and four damaged. Shortly before he left the unit he was allocated BL753 and, unusually for him, he adorned it with the name of his wife, Leola – his subsequent aircraft were unmarked. Blakeslee was at the fighter's controls when, at lunchtime on 28 April, he was in combat over the coast near Dunkirk with a number of Fw 190s – he subsequently claimed two of them probably destroyed. Blakeslee attacked one head on, and it spun down on fire, and then he hit the second one. His final claim with No 401 Sqn was also in BL753 when, on the afternoon of 30 May, he damaged another Fw 190. BL753 remained on operations until it was lost while artillery spotting over France soon after D-Day.

5

Spitfire VB EN918/AV-X of Flt Lt S R Edner, No 121 'Eagle' Sqn, Southend, July-August 1942

From July 1942 EN918 was the regular mount of Californian Selden Edner, who used it on 19 July to damage a Bf 109 in a combat fought over the Channel. On the last day of the month, over the sea off Berck-sur-Mer, Edner (again in EN918) destroyed two Bf 109Fs to take his total to four. Shortly after 0900 hrs on 19 August, he and EN918 were part of a patrol from No 121 Sqn that arrived over Dieppe to provide cover for the invasion force that was coming under attack from ever-larger formations of German bombers. The unit soon became embroiled in action, forcing its pilots to split up. No 121 Sqn duly suffered several losses, although Edner managed to destroy an Fw 190 to take him to 'acedom' – EN918 suffered a damaged tailplane during the course of the engagement. Sel Edner was awarded a DFC for his efforts at Dieppe. EN918 transferred to the USAAF and joined the 335th FS, but was lost in early 1943.

6

Spitfire VB BM635/WZ-Y of 2Lt D E Shafer Jr, 309th FS/31st FG, High Ercall, 29 June 1942

Dale Shafer was posted to England with the 31st FG in the spring of 1942, and on arrival he converted onto the Spitfire. With his squadron, Shafer continued to work up to an operational state before being committed to action. BM635 was delivered to the 309th on 21 June, and was flown by Shafer on a training sortie on the 29th, when it suffered a slight accident at High Ercall. He moved with the 31st FG to North Africa later in the year and made his initial claims over Tunisia shortly before the Axis surrender. BM635 later served with a Free French squadron and on training duties until it was scrapped in early 1945.

7
Spitfire VB (serial overpainted)/MX-A of 2Lt J H White, 307th FS/31st FG, Westhampnett, 19 August 1942

The first major action for the USAAF in Europe was the Dieppe operation on 19 August 1942, when much of the 31st FG was blooded for the first time. Among those involved was 1Lt John White of the 307th FS, who flew this aircraft over the withdrawing convoy in the late afternoon. With rain showers and low cloud covering their approach, enemy fighters continued to harass the force as it limped back to the UK. At about 1730 hrs four Fw 190s appeared out of the murk to attack, but they were spotted by pilots from the 307th, including White, who engaged them. In a brief combat, White and, it is believed, Lt Wooten hit and probably destroyed one of the Focke-Wulfs, but due to the weather they could not confirm their kill. Nonetheless, it was the first claim for John White, who went on to achieve 'acedom' flying Spitfires in the Mediterranean the following year.

8
Spitfire VB EP179/WZ-A of Maj H R Thyng, 309th FS/31st FG, Westhampnett, 22 September 1942

Maj Harry Thyng was CO of the 309th FS when it commenced operations in England in the summer of 1942, and he was credited with two damaged claims during August. At Westhampnett on 22 September, the 309th was made available for the press, during which they staged a practice scramble – Thyng used EP179, which was his own aircraft (it bore the names of his wife and son on the port side). Late in the day shortly before dusk, and although notionally now non-operational, a section of Spitfires from the 309th, led by Maj Thyng in this aircraft, was scrambled after an intruder. Off the coast in the increasing gloom, he spotted a Ju 88, which he attacked and hit, but it was then lost to view in the darkness. Thyng returned to base, but could only claim the bomber as probably destroyed.

9
Spitfire VB EN853/AV-D of Maj W J Daley, 335th FS/4th FG, Debden, October 1942

One of the leading 'Eagle' pilots, Maj Jim Daley had served with distinction in No 121 Sqn, where he had become a flight commander and made five claims, including at least 2.5 destroyed. A natural leader, upon transferring to the USAAF in September 1942, he was promoted to command the squadron, re-titled the 335th FS. This aircraft was his regular mount, and Daley is believed to have been flying it on 2 October when the 4th FG made its first claims whilst supporting a 'Circus' by USAAF B-17 Flying Fortresses. In an engagement fought at 24,000 ft over the French coast between Calais and Dunkirk, four Fw 190s were confirmed destroyed, while Daley claimed one damaged. He continued to lead his squadron until he left for the US in late November. EN853 did not last long, however, as it was shot down near St Omer by an Fw 190 in late January 1943.

10
Spitfire VB BM510/XR-A of Maj G A Daymond, 334th FS/4th FG, Debden, October 1942

'Gus' Daymond was one of the most distinguished 'Eagle' squadron pilots, rising to command No 71 Sqn – a position that he retained when the unit was transferred to the USAAF as the 334th FS. By that time he had seven victories to his name, including four in Spitfires. His last victory had been claimed in this aircraft on 27 August 1942 when it was still with No 71 Sqn, and upon joining the USAAF, Daymond retained BM510 as his personal mount. Other than the addition of US 'star' markings, in fact little changed. However, the fighter did not remain with him for long, as following an operation on 25 October, he damaged it when landing at Debden. BM510 was later repaired and transferred to the 335th FS. Maj Daymond remained in command of the 334th into the spring of 1943, but made no further claims prior to his transfer back to the US.

11
Spitfire VB BL722/MD-B of Lt J A Goodson, 336th FS/4th FG, Debden, October 1942

After service with No 222 'Natal' Sqn, BL722 joined No 133 'Eagle' Sqn and was transferred to the 336th FS in September 1942. With them, it became one of the first Spitfires to acquire decorative nose art in the form of a top hat, cane and gloves. Thus adorned, the aircraft was flown by several distinguished pilots, including future aces Lts 'Dixie' Alexander and James Goodson. The latter had previously served with an RCAF Spitfire squadron prior to joining No 133 Sqn, with whom he transferred to the USAAF. Goodson became the 336th FS's CO as it converted to the P-47, and flying these, and later the P-51, he went on to claim 14 victories. BL722 was subsequently returned to the RAF and served on training duties until finally written off in a crash in October 1944.

12
Spitfire VB BL255/MD-T of Lt D S Gentile, 336th FS/4th FG, Debden, November 1942

With 21 and 2 shared victories, Don Gentile was the 4th FG's leading ace of World War 2. His first two victories came during the Dieppe raid whilst flying Spitfires with No 133 Sqn, and the following month he transferred, along with the rest of the squadron, to the USAAF. BL255 became Gentile's personal aircraft at this time, carrying his colourful marking (which was also used by the 336th) and two victory symbols. He flew it regularly until it was damaged by another pilot when landing at the end of November. Gentile continued to fly Spitfires on offensive operations with the 4th FG into 1943, and on 12 March he made what is believed to have been the 4th FG's final claim with the British fighter when, in a combat over Audruicq, he damaged an Fw 190. After being returned to the RAF, BL255 saw further operational service and was eventually withdrawn in May 1945.

13
Spitfire VB BL545/MD-L of Capt O H Coen, 336th FS/4th FG, Debden, 22 January 1943

The last major engagement involving Spitfires of the 4th FG took place on 22 January 1943 when the 336th FS covered the second of two boxes of bombers sent to attack St Omer airfield. The Bostons bombed in turn, but on egressing the target area they were followed by more than a dozen Fw 190s from JG 26. Coen, who was flying this aircraft, led the Spitfires towards the enemy fighters, which initially turned away. The Spitfires then returned to their charges, but over the Pas de Calais area the enemy attacked, and the 336th's Spitfires once more turned into them. Coen described how 'I gave him a short burst from about 150 yards, quarter astern and white smoke came out. He then fell off on his port side and dived into the sea. The pilot did not bale out'. Oscar Coen's fifth victory made him the Eighth Air Force's first ace. BL545 was later returned to the RAF and used for gun spotting duties on D-Day.

14
Spitfire VB BL449(?)/CG-P of Lt Col C G Peterson, 4th FG, Debden, December 1942-January 1943

The serial number of this aircraft is not certain, but is believed to be BL449, which was used by ex-'Eagle' ace Lt Col 'Pete' Peterson during his time as Executive Officer of the 4th FG, which he later commanded. Peterson, who had been the first 'Eagle' to command a squadron, achieved six of his victories in the Spitfire when with No 71 Sqn. He was transferred to the USAAF as a lieutenant colonel, and followed the RAF practice for Wing Leaders to have their initials carried on their personal aircraft in place of unit code letters. This aircraft is believed to have been the very first USAAF fighter to have worn a personal code. If CG-P was indeed BL449, then it was transferred back to the British in early 1943 and eventually passed on to Portugal.

15
Spitfire IX BS513/PK-Z of Capt F S Gabreski, No 315 'Deblinski' Sqn, Northolt, January-February 1943

The leading American ace in the European theatre, 'Gabby' Gabreski made all his claims flying the formidable P-47. However, his operational debut came with one of the RAF's Polish-manned Spitfire squadrons. Of Polish extraction, in December 1942 Gabreski was attached to the veteran No 315 Sqn based at Northolt under the command of Sqn Ldr Tadeusz Sawicz, who at that time had five claims (including three kills), in order to gain some operational experience. Gabreski completed his first 'Circus' mission on 21 January, and during his brief stay with the Poles flew this aircraft on several operations during January and February, until he joined the 56th FG at the end of that month. BS513 served with several other Polish units and survived the war to become an instructional airframe.

16
Spitfire VC BR112/X of Plt Off C Weaver RCAF, No 185 Sqn, Ta Kali, Malta, 9 September 1942

With 12.5 victories to his credit, Claude Weaver from Oklahoma was the second most successful American Spitfire pilot. Most of his kills were achieved when serving with the RAF in Malta during a hectic six-week period in the summer of 1942. During early September No 185 Sqn flew offensive sorties over Sicily, and in the mid-morning of the 9th Weaver was flying this aircraft on a sweep when his unit was engaged by half-a-dozen C.202s of the 352° *Squadriglia*. 'Weavy' went after one and was last seen following it in a near vertical dive. He then called up on the radio claiming a kill, but his Spitfire had also been hit and set on fire by a second Macchi fighter. Weaver was forced to crash-land on a Sicilian beach, and thus became a PoW, although he later

escaped. His aircraft had the lighter part of its camouflage overpainted to make it better suited for use over the dark waters of the Mediterranean.

17
Spitfire VC BR390/ZX-N of Flt Sgt MacA Powers, No 145 Sqn, LG 173, Egypt, 2 November 1942

MacArthur Powers began his air combat career during service with the RAF in the bitter air fighting over the desert around the time of the Battle of El Alamein. His first confirmed victory was claimed at the start of that great battle, and during an early morning patrol on 2 November he was again at the controls of this aircraft over Rhaz el Shaqiq as the Allied breakout began. With the battle raging below him, Powers engaged a Bf 109, which he damaged. The following afternoon, when part of an eight-aircraft patrol over Daba, the American shared in the destruction of a Bf 109. He made his final Spitfire claim near Fuka late the next morning when his section surprised a trio of Bf 109s and he shot one of them down. Following transfer to the USAAF, Powers was credited with five victories while flying P-40s.

18
Spitfire VC ES252/ZX-E of Sqn Ldr L C Wade, No 145 Sqn, Bu Grara, Tunisia, March 1943

Claiming 10 of his 22 and 2 shared victories with the Spitfire, Lance Wade was one of the most successful American exponents of the type. All his earlier victories were achieved in Hurricanes, but in early 1943 he joined No 145 Sqn, which he was soon promoted to command. Wade claimed his first Spitfire victory at the beginning of March, and he used this aircraft on the 8th to damage a Bf 109. Then, over Mareth on the 21st, again whilst flying ES252, he engaged another Bf 109, which he claimed as a probable. In the same area the following day, again in this aircraft, Weaver shot down a Bf 109 to claim his second Spitfire victory, and by the end of the Tunisian campaign he had destroyed six more Axis fighters. Moving with the squadron to Italy, Wade made further claims, until he left No 145 Sqn after being promoted to wing commander in November 1943. He was killed in a flying accident two months later.

19
Spitfire VC EP829/T-N of Sqn Ldr J J Lynch, No 249 Sqn, Qrendi, Malta, April 1943

Having served in England with No 71 'Eagle' Sqn in 1942, Californian John Lynch transferred to Malta and No 249 Sqn in November of that year. His score soon mounted, and he became an ace in mid-December. In March 1943 Lynch took command of No 249 Sqn, and he claimed his first victory in this aircraft on 7 April when he shot down a Ju 88. Towards the end of the month, again in EP829, he met with great success targeting enemy transport aircraft trying to support the fighting in Tunisia. Indeed, between the 22nd and 28th Lynch claimed 4.5 transports destroyed, with the Ju 52/3m that he shot down on the latter date being assessed as the 1000th victim of the Malta squadrons. Flying another aircraft, Lynch shot down three more transports in early May. His final victory came over Sicily in July 1943, taking his total to 17 (ten and seven shared) victories, and thus making him the most successful American Spitfire pilot of them all.

20

Spitfire VC ER570/WD-Q of Maj R Levine, 4th FS/52nd FG, La Sers, Tunisia, April 1943

The 4th FS's CO from mid-1942 was Robert Levine, who was promoted to major on 1 January 1943 and who led the unit through much of the North African campaign. A respected leader, he scored his own, and his squadron's, first success in early January when he used ER570 to shoot down an Fw 190 – this victory was duly recorded on the nose of the aircraft. Like other Spitfires of the 4th FS at the time, ER570 carried its pilot's name in script, as well as Maj Levine's striking skull marking. He was also flying this aircraft on 19 April when, over La Sebala, he shot down a Bf 109. Levine's third, and final, victory came the next day when he bagged another Messerschmitt, probably from II./JG 51. These kills, plus one probable, were all claimed in ER570. In February 1944 Levine was made group commander of the 52nd FG, while ER570 was later returned to the RAF and eventually scrapped in early 1945.

21

Spitfire IX EN447/WD-L of Lt V N Cabas, 4th FS/52nd FG, Le Sers, Tunisia, 19 April 1943

Having claimed his first victory over Dieppe with the RCAF, Vic Cabas then transferred to the USAAF and joined the 52nd FG's 4th FS. He moved to North Africa, where, over Tunisia in the spring of 1943, he achieved considerable success. When the squadron was issued with a small number of Spitfire IXs, Cabas was allocated one as 'his' aircraft, which he named "KAY II" and decorated with his score. He is believed to have been flying it on 19 April when, during a combat to the north of Tunis, he and 1Lt John Blythe shared in the destruction of a Bf 109. This proved to be Cabas' final claim, as his tour ended soon afterwards. Interestingly, his aircraft retained RAF wing and tail markings.

22

Spitfire VC (serial overpainted)/MX-Y of Lt J D Collinsworth, 307th FS/31st FG, La Sers, Tunisia, 6 May 1943

One of the 31st FG's great characters, Jerry Collinsworth was flying his personally-marked aircraft on 6 May 1943 when the group met with considerable success over Tunis. Wingman to Maj La Brecht, Collinsworth spotted a pair of Fw 190s, and pulling up behind the trailing fighter, he fired at it. Moments later its canopy flew off and the pilot baled out. Hauling his Spitfire, nicknamed *Dimples II*, around, Collinsworth found the sky empty, save for the billowing white parachute of his victim. As he flew by, he opened the canopy and 'thumbed his nose' at him! Collinsworth then headed for home. He reached 'acedom' the following month, before returning to the US later in the year.

23

Spitfire VC ER187/WZ-C of Maj F A Hill, 309th FS/31st FG, La Sers, Tunisia, 6 May 1943

Having reached 'acedom' during a morning sortie on 6 May 1943, later that day Maj Frank Hill led another sweep in ER187, which was his personally-marked Spitfire VC. Over Tunis, the unit found a mixed formation of Bf 109s and C.202s, and Hill immediately attacked. He fired at, and hit,

one of the Macchis, which rolled away. He then became embroiled in a general dogfight, and after firing at a Bf 109, he had the satisfaction of seeing it dive away, before engaging another fighter. Eventually, out of ammunition and short on fuel, Hill and his wingman disengaged and headed home – he was later credited with one destroyed and two damaged. Hill, whose final victory the following month took his total to seven, later commanded the 31st FG until September, when he returned to the US.

24

Spitfire VC ES276/WD-D of 1Lt S Feld, 4th FS/52nd FG, La Sebala, Tunisia, June 1943

Sylvan Feld was one of the leading, but least known, USAAF aces to fly the Spitfire, and he was regarded as being so ferocious that he sometimes unnerved his own colleagues! Between March and June 1943, he destroyed nine enemy aircraft, which were recorded on the nose of his regular Spitfire VC, ES276. Interestingly, unlike most USAAF Spitfires, this combat-weary machine was marked up in the Type B desert colour scheme. ES276 was later used by the 309th FS, and eventually returned to the RAF to be scrapped in 1946. Unlike his aircraft, however, 'Sid' Feld did not survive the war, being shot down by flak over Normandy flying P-47Ds with the 373rd FG on 13 August 1944, and then falling victim to a USAAF bombing raid whilst a PoW in Bernay one week later.

25

Spitfire IX (serial overpainted)/QP-N of Lt F Ohr, 2nd FS/52nd FG, Palermo, Sicily, August 1943

On 9 April 1943, Fred Ohr, who hailed from Oregon, was participating in a 52nd FG sweep over Tunisia when his formation encountered a large number of unescorted Ju 88s. In a one-sided fight, six of the Junkers bombers fell to the guns of the American Spitfires, including one to Ohr, who claimed his first, and only, victory in the British fighter. Serving with the 2nd FS throughout its sojourn in the Mediterranean, he often flew this aircraft (painted in the RAF's high altitude fighter scheme) on local patrols and ground attack missions when based in Sicily. Fred Ohr became the only USAAF ace of Korean ancestry during the summer of 1944 when he claimed five more victories following his conversion to the P-51.

26

Spitfire VC JK550/JS-C of Lt Col J S Coward, 52nd FG, Palermo, Sicily, August 1943

Lt Col James Coward, who was a well-respected fighter leader, assumed command of the 52nd FG at La Sebala, in Tunisia, on 20 June 1943 after his predecessor was injured. He remained in the post until the end of August, having led the group to Sicily the previous month. Coward was an experienced Spitfire operator following time with the 2nd FS, which he had commanded from 13 September 1942 through to 20 June 1943. On 30 November 1942, whilst patrolling over Teboura, Coward and his wingman engaged a pair of Bf 109s in what proved to be the 2nd FS's first engagement with the enemy. Both aircraft were shot down, with one falling to Coward, who thus registered his only victory. Like most group commanders, he used his initials to identify his aircraft in true British style. Following its return to the RAF in the spring of 1944, JK550 saw further operational service in Italy, and was eventually transferred to the French *Armee de l'Air* in 1946.

27

Spitfire VC JK777/QP-Z of 1Lt R L Alexander, 2nd FS/ 52nd FG, Bocca di Falco, Sicily, August-September 1943

'Dixie' Alexander was one of the more colourful former 'Eagle' squadron pilots to join the 52nd FG in the Mediterranean in July 1943, having made his initial claims with the RAF. Upon joining the 2nd FS, Alexander was frustrated to find that his group was confined to defensive duties, and he first flew this aircraft on one such sortie (a patrol lasting 1 hour and 35 minutes) over Palermo harbour on 17 August. He flew it again several times on similar missions in early September. Like other 2nd FS Spitfires, JK777 was marked with the unit's *American Beagle Sqdn* badge on the nose. When he was later allocated his own aircraft, Alexander decorated it with several markings, including a striking sharksmouth. He made two more claims flying Spitfires in early 1944, and eventually became an ace flying P-51Bs, before being shot down in error by a B-24 gunner over the Austrian town of Aschbach during an escort mission on 30 May 1944. He spent the rest of the war as a PoW. JK777 was later transferred back to the RAF and flew with No 185 Sqn from Malta.

28

Spitfire VIII JF452/FA-H of Col F A Hill, 31st FG, Termini and Milazzo, Sicily, September 1943

On 13 July 1943, two days after making his final claim, Frank Hill was promoted to command the 31st FG. He initially inherited the Spitfire IX (EN329) flown by his predecessor, Col Fred Dean, who had adopted the RAF practice of senior officers personalising their aircraft by identifying them with their initials, rather than unit codes. Frank Hill continued the practice, and the Spitfire IX he took over eventually carried his initials. By early September he was flying superb new Spitfire VIII JF452, which bore his initials, his substantial score and both his and his wife's names. This aircraft, which was camouflaged in standard desert colours, was flown by Hill for the latter part of his time as CO of the 31st FG, which he led with great success throughout the Sicilian campaign. He made no further aerial claims with it, however. Hill duly passed the aircraft on to his successor, Col Charles McCorkle (see profile 30) .

29

Spitfire VC (serial overpainted)/WZ-S of 1Lt G G Loving, 309th FS/31st FG, Pomigliano, Italy, December 1943

After having flown some 25 combat missions, 2Lt George Loving was allocated this aircraft, which he described as 'a well worn Mk V' in late December 1943. In honour of his girlfriend, he named it *Ginger*, and had the name painted on the nose. The aircraft was also unusual in having dark (possibly olive) green uppersurfaces. When over Cassino a few days after the fighter was allocated to Loving, a fragment of an 88 mm flak shell shattered *Ginger's* windscreen, but caused no other damage. Loving continued to regularly fly this aircraft during the early part of 1944, including covering

patrols over the Anzio beachhead, although such missions were increasingly flown by Spitfire IXs. He may have been flying WZ-S when he was involved in a combat with six Bf 109s during a bomber escort mission in the final weeks of the 31st FG's service with the Spitfire, sharing in the destruction of one of them. Loving converted to the Mustang soon afterwards, and 'made ace' with five victories in the American fighter. The original 'Ginger' remained a part of his life, however, as he married her shortly after returning to America!

30

Spitfire VIII JF452/CM-M of Col C M McCorkle, 31st FG, Castel Volturno, Italy, January-February 1944

'Sandy' McCorkle assumed leadership of the 31st FG from Frank Hill in mid September 1943, and he also inherited the latter's Spitfire VIII, which, although the serial was overpainted, was probably JF452. McCorkle claimed his first victory (an Me 210) on 30 September, and on 6 January he almost certainly used this aircraft to down his third (an Fw 190). A month later, once more it is thought in his personal Mk VIII, he claimed his fifth and last on the Spitfire. As well as his initials, McCorkle's Spitfire carried his wife's name on the nose, as well as the 31st FG badge, under the windscreen.

31

Spitfire VIII (serial overpainted)/HL-X of 1Lt L P Molland, 308th FS/31st FG, Castel Volturno, Italy, February 1944

In little more than a month in early 1944, 24-year-old North Dakotan 'Tommy' Molland claimed four and one shared victories, plus one probable, flying Spitfires in the bitter air fighting after the Anzio landings. He had been allocated this aircraft in early 1944, and he decorated it with a caricature of a Wells Fargo stagecoach and the nickname *FARGO Express*. The fighter carried Molland's score beneath the windscreen, with his confirmed victories in black and probables in white. Molland converted with the rest of the group onto the P-51B, and he used the American fighter to claim a further six kills. He also became CO of the 308th FS at the end of July 1944.

32

Spitfire XVI TB752/KH-Z of Sqn Ldr H P M Zary RCAF, No 403 Sqn RCAF, B114 Diepholz, Germany, 21 April 1945

Sqn Ldr Henry Zary, who hailed from New York, served throughout the war with the RCAF. During the fighting over Normandy after D-Day he claimed four victories flying with No 421 Sqn, including three Bf 109s in one sortie. In early 1945 Zary joined No 403 Sqn as its CO, and he led the unit on armed reconnaissance sorties over the shrinking Reich in the final hectic months of the war. During the late afternoon of 21 April, Zary was flying this Spitfire XVI when he shot down a Bf 109 near Schnackenburg to become the final American Spitfire ace of World War 2. Four days later, whilst being flown by another pilot, TB752 shot down its second enemy aircraft, and the fighter claimed its third kill when yet another pilot destroyed an Fw 190. The aircraft survived the war and is now on display at the Spitfire Memorial Museum at Manston, in Kent. Sadly, however, Henry Zary died of natural causes in Quebec, Canada, following a short illness on 11 February 1946.

Bibliography

Alexander, Capt Richard L, *They Called Me Dixie.* Robinson Typo, 1988

Caine, Brig Gen Philip D, *American Pilots in the RAF.* Brassey (US), 1993

Chandler, Maj Clifford H, *USAAF Spitfire Operations in the Mediterranean.* Private (USAF Air Command & Staff College, Maxwell AFB)

Cull, Brian, *249 at War,* Grub St, 1997

Cull, Brian & Galea, Frederick, *Spitfires over Malta.* Grub St, 2005

Cull, Brian et al, *Spitfires over Sicily.* Grub St, 2001

Donahue, Flt Lt A G, DFC, *Last Flight From Singapore.* Macmillan, 1944

Flintham, Vic & Thomas, Andrew, *Combat Codes.* Airlife, 2003

Franks, Norman, *Beyond Courage.* Grub St, 2003

Fry, Garry L & Ethell, Jeffery L, *Escort to Berlin.* Arco Publishing, 1980

Goodson James A & Franks, Norman, *Over-Paid, Over-Sexed and Over Here.* Wingham Press, 1991

Halley, James, *Squadrons of the RAF & Commonwealth.* Air Britain, 1988

Haughland, Verne, *The Eagle Squadrons.* David and Charles, 1979

Holmes, Tony, *American Eagles.* Classic Publications, 2001

Jefford, Wg Cdr C G, *RAF Squadrons.* Airlife, 1988 & 2001

Kucera, Dennis C, *In a Now Forgotten Sky.* Flying Machines Press, 1997

McIntosh, Dave, *High Blue Battle.* Spa Books, 1990

Milberry, Larry & Halliday, Hugh, *The RCAF at War 1939-1945.* CANAV, 1990

Olynyk, Frank, *Stars and Bars.* Grub St, 1995

Rawlings, John D R, *Fighter Squadrons of the RAF.* Macdonald, 1969

Rogers, Anthony, *185 – The Malta Squadron.* Spellmount, 2005

Shores, Christopher, *Aces High Vol 2.* Grub St, 1999

Shores, Christopher & Cull, Brian with Maliza, Nicola, *Malta – the Spitfire Year – 1942.* Grub St, 1988

Shores, Christopher & Ring, Hans, *Fighters over the Desert.* Neville Spearman, 1969

Shores, Christopher & Williams, Clive, *Aces High Vol 1.* Grub St, 1994

Shores, Christopher, Ring, Hans & Hess, William, *Fighters over Tunisia.* Neville Spearman, 1974

Sturtivant, Ray et al, *Spitfire International.* Air Britain, 2002

Acknowledgements

The author is grateful to the Public Affairs Officers of the 31st FW, based at Aviano, in Italy, and the 52nd FW, based at Spangdahlem, in Germany, for their generous help in providing information and images for this volume. SMSgt Daniel Wheaton of the Air Force Historical Research Agency at Maxwell AFB provided combat reports and other contemporary accounts from USAF records, while further material was provided by Chris Hobson of the Joint Services Command and Staff College at Shrivenham. Other friends and fellow enthusiasts have also been most generous in providing material, notably Brian Cull, Robert Forsyth, Norman Franks, Harry Holmes, Peter Green, Wojtek Matusiak, Frank Olynyk, Jerry Scutts, Chris Shores and Chris Thomas.

INDEX

References to illustrations are shown in **bold**. Plates are shown with page and caption locators in (brackets).